THE ROAD TO
SUCCESS
With MTSS

A **Ten-Step Process** for Schools

TOM HIERCK **&** CHRIS WEBER

Solution Tree | Press
a division of
Solution Tree

555 North Morton Street
Bloomington, IN 47404
800.733.6786 (toll free) / 812.336.7700
FAX: 812.336.7790

email: info@SolutionTree.com
SolutionTree.com

Visit **go.SolutionTree.com/schoolimprovement** to download the free reproducibles in this book.

Printed in the United States of America

Library of Congress Cataloging-in-Publication Data

Names: Hierck, Tom, 1960- author. | Weber, Chris (Chris A.), author.
Title: The road to success with MTSS : a ten-step process for schools / Tom
    Hierck, Chris Weber.
Description: Bloomington, IN : Solution Tree Press, 2022. | Includes
    bibliographical references and index.
Identifiers: LCCN 2022006883 (print) | LCCN 2022006884 (ebook) | ISBN
    9781954631373 (paperback) | ISBN 9781954631380 (ebook)
Subjects: LCSH: Student growth (Academic achievement)--United States. |
    School assistance programs--United States. | Individualized
    instruction--United States. | Learning strategies--United States. |
    Behavior modification--United States. | Response to intervention
    (Learning disabled children)--United States.
Classification: LCC LB1062.6 .H53 2022 (print) | LCC LB1062.6 (ebook) |
    DDC 371.39/4--dc23/eng/20220315
LC record available at https://lccn.loc.gov/2022006883
LC ebook record available at https://lccn.loc.gov/2022006884

Solution Tree
Jeffrey C. Jones, CEO
Edmund M. Ackerman, President

Solution Tree Press
President and Publisher: Douglas M. Rife
Associate Publisher: Sarah Payne-Mills
Managing Production Editor: Kendra Slayton
Editorial Director: Todd Brakke
Art Director: Rian Anderson
Copy Chief: Jessi Finn
Senior Production Editor: Tonya Maddox Cupp
Content Development Specialist: Amy Rubenstein
Proofreader: Sarah Ludwig
Text and Cover Designer: Kelsey Hoover
Associate Editor: Sarah Ludwig
Editorial Assistants: Charlotte Jones and Elijah Oates

DEDICATIONS

As I enter my fortieth year as an educator, I remain grateful to all who have contributed to my growth and knowledge acquisition. This includes my colleagues in their roles as support staff, teachers, and leaders; the many students I've been fortunate to teach and connect with; my friends and community members who have always been willing to share feedback; and my family, who always are there to remind me about what's most important and what matters most. Thanks to each and every one of you.

—Tom Hierck

I dedicate this book to Nana Ito, the best person, parent, friend, and educator I've ever known.

—Chris Weber

ACKNOWLEDGMENTS

Collectively, we have written nearly twenty books with Solution Tree. There is no better partner for an author or consultant than Solution Tree. Guided by Jeff Jones, we believe Solution Tree is the preeminent educational publishing and professional development company in the world. There is no finer man or publisher than Solution Tree Press President, Douglas Rife, and we thank him for decades of support. Thanks to Tonya Cupp and Sarah Payne-Mills for their outstanding support in editing this book; no one supports an author in creating a book better than Solution Tree. We cannot thank the professional development and events departments at Solution Tree, led by Shannon Ritz, Renee Marshall, and Debbie Hennessey, enough for supporting us and others as we share our passion and ideas with colleagues around the world. We hope this book moves Solution Tree one step closer to achieving its vision of transforming education worldwide.

Finally, we believe that Rick and Becky DuFour were the most innovative, transformational, and significant educators in the United States since Benjamin Bloom; we miss them and we honor their work. Every idea in this book rests on the foundation of Professional Learning Communities (PLCs) at Work®, and no practice in this book will be successful or sustained without a collaborative commitment to all students by all staff. We look forward to a day when PLCs are not something we do but simply who we are.

Solution Tree Press would like to thank the following reviewers:

Chad Dumas
Educational Consultant
Next Learning Solutions
Ames, Iowa

John D. Ewald
Solution Tree Associate
Former Superintendent, Principal,
  Teacher
Frederick, Maryland

Janet Gilbert
Principal
Mountain Shadows Elementary School
Glendale, Arizona

Melissa Martinez Saenz
Principal
Montwood Middle School
El Paso, Texas

Melisha Plummer
Assistant Principal
South Atlanta High School
Atlanta, Georgia

Vanessa Cevallos Reyes
Principal
Sam Rayburn High School
Pasadena, Texas

Jason Salhaney
Principal
Owen Intermediate School
Belleville, Michigan

Ringnolda Jofee' Tremain
PK3–8 Principal
Trinity Basin Preparatory
Fort Worth, Texas

Steven Weber
Associate Superintendent for Teaching
  and Learning
Fayetteville Public Schools
Fayetteville, Arkansas

Gail Whisnant
Assistant Principal
Cleveland County Schools
Lawndale, North Carolina

Visit **go.SolutionTree.com/schoolimprovement** to download the free reproducibles in this book.

TABLE OF CONTENTS

Reproducibles are in italics.

CHAPTER 5

What Does Student Evidence Reveal?

Epilogue

APPENDIX

Case Studies

References and Resources

Index

ABOUT THE AUTHORS

Tom Hierck has been an educator since 1983 in a career that has spanned all grade levels and many roles in public education. His experiences as a teacher, an administrator, a district leader, a department of education project leader, and an executive director provide a unique context for his education philosophy.

Tom is a compelling presenter, infusing his message of hope with strategies culled from the real world. He understands that educators face unprecedented challenges and knows which strategies will best serve learning communities. Tom has presented to schools and districts across North America with a message of celebration for educators seeking to make a difference in the lives of students. His dynamic presentations explore the importance of positive learning environments and the role of assessment to improve student learning. Tom's belief that "every student is a success story waiting to be told" has led him to work with teachers and administrators to create positive school cultures and build effective relationships that facilitate learning for all students.

To learn more about Tom's work, visit his website at tomhierck.com, or follow @thierck on Twitter or Tom Hierck on Facebook.

Chris Weber, EdD, is an expert in behavior, mathematics, response to intervention (RTI), and multitiered system of supports (MTSS) who consults and presents internationally to audiences on important topics in education. As a teacher, principal, and curriculum director in California and Illinois, Chris worked with his colleagues to develop systems of supports that have led to high levels of learning at schools across the United States. In addition to writing and consulting, he continues to work in Irvine Unified School District in California, supporting some of the best and highest-performing schools in the country. Chris has been in service to community and country his entire life. A graduate of the U.S. Air Force Academy, he flew C-141s during his military career. He is also a former high school, middle school, and elementary school teacher and administrator. To learn more about Chris's work, visit Chris Weber Education (https://chriswebereducation.com) or follow @WeberEducation on Twitter.

To book Tom Hierck or Chris Weber for professional development, contact pd@ SolutionTree.com.

INTRODUCTION

Multitiered system of supports (MTSS) is about using the knowledge, skills, and attributes of all members of a learning organization to positively impact the life chances of all students. It is common sense in action. Citing Felipe Mercado (2018), Matt Navo and Amy Williams (2023) suggest, "fundamentally, MTSS involves designing learning opportunities that maximize inclusivity and access for all students while minimizing barriers and structures that marginalize individual students or groups, and it provides a framework supporting educators' efforts to address disparities between student groups" (p. 4). This framework involves an exciting and dramatic redesign of general and special education for continuously improved student outcomes (Buffum, Mattos, & Weber, 2012; Hierck, Coleman, & Weber, 2011).

We also often see that MTSS and response to intervention (RTI) get used interchangeably. While they share some common thinking, they are fundamentally different in some key ways. RTI is generally approached as a model for identifying and addressing the specific academic needs of struggling students. MTSS is defined as having a much broader scope to the degree that, while academic needs are addressed, so are nonacademic social and emotional areas, including behavior. MTSS in schools and districts may also include school culture, the role of family and community in supporting the initiatives, and structuring teacher professional development to support the outcomes. It is a school- or districtwide construct that ensures high-quality instruction and research-based systematic interventions for all student needs—behavioral (including social-emotional) and academic.

We believe that school administrators and their staffs *want* to do MTSS and know they *need* to do MTSS. This belief is based on our more than sixty years of combined experience as educators at all grade levels working with students across the behavioral and academic spectrum. Between us, we have worked with United

States educators in the vast majority of the fifty states and also with educators in every province and territory in Canada. Gaining insight into what works, what needs to be adjusted, and what needs to be abandoned has allowed us to collaborate in hundreds of schools with thousands of educators to create localized, contextualized responses that stand the best chance of being both sustainable and successful. Our work in the field has highlighted for us that school teams frequently don't know what they need to do and don't know where to start. Educators want and need someone to craft a model *with* them, a model that ensures high-quality instruction and research-based systematic interventions for all student needs and ultimately results in all students learning at high levels.

Our experiences are the motivation behind the MTSS road map—a customized strategic solution that recognizes that each school is unique and that a uniquely developed MTSS plan is necessary. We liken this to you and your team embarking on a road trip to becoming the school you seek to become. As with any journey, there will be key considerations involved in planning for the trip, key milestones along the journey, potential new learning at some of the stopping points, and an overall satisfaction at arriving at your destination. The intent is to help you craft a solution that is contextualized to your school and that matches its mission and vision. The emphasis is on *transformational learning*—which generates long-term change and benefits and may affect learners' future experiences—as opposed to *transactional learning*, which occurs in a moment or for a specific purpose and doesn't necessarily connect to future learning (Wenger, 2014).

Why MTSS Is Crucial

From struggling students striving to meet minimum proficiency to gifted students seeking to reach their potential, MTSS invites a partnership among students, teachers, parents, and the community whereby all students achieving positive behavioral, social-emotional, and academic outcomes is the priority.

We have too often lowered our expectations, in most cases subconsciously, on the basis of socioeconomic status, ethnicity, number of parents, or some other external variable (Cherng, 2017). Sometimes it's our big hearts that override the logic, and we lower expectations while believing we are positively supporting the student who struggles for some of these reasons. MTSS has the power to address and ameliorate these historical injustices. We believe that schools can and absolutely will make a difference in the lives of *all* students.

We have learned another critical lesson across the decades: developing a plan—even implementing a plan—is not enough. The plan must result in improved student outcomes. Evidence is paramount to MTSS, as data drive decisions.

Take a moment to think about a student who challenges you the most (behaviorally, academically, social-emotionally, or some of all of these) and what the future holds for that student if the educators and leaders at your school don't collectively and systematically provide supports that result in positive outcomes. As challenging as that student might be, what options remain open if his or her behaviors result in consequential responses only from the adults? If any of the current supports you and your team provide in school are removed, such as those identified in Tiers 2 and 3 of the MTSS model, how will that student make any gains in those areas where currently deficient?

It becomes readily predictable to see that the absence of the supports currently in place would result in further gaps in learning, which often results in further disruptive behavior, ultimately leading to a parting of the ways and either an alternative school setting offered or the student dropping out. Many readers are familiar with the United States's pipeline-to-prison scenario. The information in figure I.1 provides a bleak outlook about the likely outcomes for dropouts. Canada's dropout rate varies greatly by province and socioeconomics, with an average rate between 5 percent and 14 percent (though the rate is as high as 50 percent in low-income areas; Pathways to Education, 2019). The disparities between those who do not finish high school and those who do are similar to those experienced in the United States.

United States	
Total number of high school dropouts annually	1,200,000
Number of high school students who drop out each day	7,000
Percent of Americans with a high school diploma	85.3%
Percent of all dropouts that happen in the ninth grade	36%
Percent of students who repeat ninth grade that go on to graduate	15%
Percent of students in largest fifty U.S. cities that graduate from high school	59%
Percent of U.S. crimes committed by a high school dropout	75%
Difference in lifetime income between high school graduate and dropout	$260,000
Percent of U.S. jobs for which a high school dropout is ineligible	90%

Source: DoSomething.org, n.d.

Figure I.1: High school dropout statistics.

These realities highlight the moral imperative to ensure that all students achieve at least a high school diploma. In the effort to significantly improve these numbers, MTSS is shown to move schools toward increased graduation rates (Brown-Chidsey & Bickford, 2016; Hall & Mahoney, 2013; Hattie, 2012; Maier et al., 2016).

How to Gear Up for MTSS: Components and Practices

Using MTSS to meet compliance audits, to raise a school's test scores by taking struggling students out of the mainstream, or to rationalize a view that students are less able or more challenging completely undermines the value of the work and reduces it to just another fad.

To implement with fidelity, it is important to know MTSS's critical components.

- High-quality instruction and learning opportunities for all students (Tier 1)
- Early identification of students struggling to meet grade-level expectations
- Attention to the learning rates and performance levels of all students
- Increased intensity and targeted instruction and intervention based on identified student needs
- Data-informed decision making using team skills to solve problems

The process of MTSS involves (1) screening for students at risk, (2) monitoring the responsiveness of students to instruction and intervention, and (3) problem solving to determine the appropriate course of action. The latter two steps of the process are repeated as needed until students are positively responding, gaps and needs are consistently met, and success is achieved and sustained. Table I.1 provides a quick review of the three tiers of intervention.

Targeted intervention *supplements*—it does not *replace*—Tier 1 instruction. Student response to supports and interventions is used to determine further course of action. If students respond to the intervention, supports are continued until gaps are eliminated. If students do not respond in a timely manner, students are provided with a different set of supports. Their progress is again monitored and further actions determined.

TABLE I.1: MTSS TIERS

Tier 1
Engaging, differentiated instruction for *all* students

- Deliver high-quality, differentiated instruction to all students.
- Provide scaffolded access to concepts and scaffolded practice of new skills.
- Issue immediate corrective feedback.
- Offer multiple opportunities to respond to instruction.
- Conduct cumulative review of previously taught skills.
- Provide small-group supports to homogenous student groups based on need.

Tier 2
More time and differentiated supports for students who have not mastered the essentials, as measured by regular assessments designed to inform instruction

- Ensure students master prioritized grade-level or course content.
- Provide time during daily thirty-minute flex times or during buffer days (days inserted into the planning calendar between units of instruction).
- Group students homogeneously during flex times, based on the behavioral and academic learning targets for which there is evidence of need.
- Staff may join grade-level teachers to reduce teacher-student ratio during flex times.
- Schools may choose to stagger times during which each grade level or course has flex time (to make optimal use of additional staff).

Tier 3
For students who have been screened to be multiple grade levels behind their peers in foundational skills (and for students who have not responded to Tier 1 and Tier 2 supports)

- Provide intensive supports in *addition* to Tier 1 and 2 supports; is informed by the evidence gathered in Tier 2.
- Provide additional supports that are as targeted as possible (for example, on phonemic awareness, single-syllable phonics, or multisyllabic phonics).
- Can temporarily occur in place of other important content but not at the expense of the target content. (For example, a student is not pulled out of Tier 1 mathematics instruction to receive Tier 3 instruction.)
- Support adjusted to match student needs and revised until student adequately responds to supports.

Designing and implementing supports for students is not easy, especially since students enter our schools and classrooms with different learning styles, readiness levels, and interests. Success at all three tiers depends on the following.

- We can prepare with differentiated and scaffolded instruction to meet students' behavioral, social-emotional, and academic needs. That's Tier 1.

- We can anticipate that not all students will learn essential behavioral and academic skills the first time we teach them or in the first way that we teach them. We can prepare with evidence-gathering opportunities—assessments—that reveal these students and their needs and embed time during which these additional, timely supports in meeting grade-level expectations can be provided. That's Tier 2.

- We can anticipate that some students have significant behavioral and academic needs and gaps in prerequisite knowledge from several grade levels or courses prior to the current grade level or course. We can prepare with timely, intensive, and targeted interventions that meet these needs. That's Tier 3.

Each tier has a lot of moving parts, so we need a system—MTSS—that organizes and sustains these tiers of support. This ensures that students who are struggling are identified in a proactive and timely manner, and teams determine early intervention solutions to minimize the impact of struggles. This information is gained by assessing student response to high-quality instruction that has been demonstrated to be effective. MTSS emphasizes outcomes. It is equally impactful for students who are not identified as struggling but who are considered gifted or above level, but whose needs may not be met.

Effective road maps present understandable steps that lead travelers to critical decision points. A road map sets clear future objectives and answers the critical why, what, and how questions to create a plan for reaching that objective. The "why" questions define objectives and strategies, the "what" questions are about challenges, solutions, and performance targets, and the "how" questions outline the processes and resources (human and technical) that will be needed along the way. With these questions answered, teams can develop their action plans. This book is structured around key parts, presented as chapters, of a successful journey.

Who This Book Is for and How This Book Is Organized

This road map provides guidance to K–12 educators—classroom teachers, special education teachers, paraprofessionals, principals, and superintendents—while suggesting when and how to make midcourse adjustments. The school principal is the key leader in the problem-solving and assessment process, and in the entire multitiered system of supports for students needing intensive intervention (students who are not responding to Tier 1 and 2 supports and identified with significant deficits in foundational skills). The principal drives the process, asking key questions, holding staff accountable, and ensuring that required resources are allocated.

The principal and the rest of the school's educators are assumed to be working as a well-functioning professional learning community (PLC). The collaborative teams that make up a PLC are a fundamental component of MTSS and are primary drivers on the journey to implement and sustain an MTSS program. There is no MTSS without PLCs, and schools in which collaborative teams are a robust, healthy, and consistent presence are likely to possess or are poised to possess a robust, healthy, and impactful multitiered system of supports. PLC processes enhance teams' capacities to meet student needs.

At the district level, superintendents and their boards might consider using the MTSS road map to vertically and horizontally align their schools across the entire K–12 system. This requires a discussion that could potentially include gaining consensus among stakeholders about shifting the distribution of resources to address the greatest areas of need in the system. At a minimum, this would be an annual discussion and could well become part of the financial planning districts engage in.

Take the following factors into consideration when beginning a journey using the MTSS road map.

- **What's our destination?** Chapter 1 describes the essential elements of successful MTSS—where you want to go—and the appendix offers case studies of implementation plans so readers can see where other schools have gone.

- **Where do we go next?** Chapter 2 explains Tiers 2 and 3 so readers know where to go when students aren't getting everything they need from Tier 1, and chapter 3 reveals what readers need to assess before and during MTSS implementation so readers know where to go next.

- **How do we get there?** Chapter 4 offers the ten steps to MTSS success and helps readers anticipate roadblocks.

- **What are our gauges telling us?** Chapter 5 explains what information schools need to make an informed decision about their journey; with this information, readers can gather and use data to inform and sustain MTSS and student success.

Think about these and their order as you would think about the steps you would engage in when planning any journey. You can ensure a successful (and enjoyable) outcome by identifying the endpoint, the stops along the way, and the best route to take, as well as by checking key indicators. The same is true of the journey to developing and enhancing your MTSS approach. The order of each chapter will effectively and efficiently guide schools in their initial or ongoing MTSS efforts. The following sections address each chapter's approach.

Chapter 1: What Practices and Elements Make Up Tier 1?

Every successful journey has a most important aspect. Maybe it's the car you're driving, the extra legroom on the flight, or the accommodations. In education—specifically in a well-defined MTSS plan—the most important aspect is the school's Tier 1 instruction and assessment practices for behavior and academics. A standards-driven, well-defined Tier 1 informs all of MTSS. It is the piece that determines whether MTSS efforts will lead to success.

A deep understanding of mapping, instruction, and assessment in academic and behavioral domains will ensure more students learn at a deeper level during core blocks of instruction. Without addressing equity and access in core programs; without focused, viable, and well-defined curricular units; and without collaborative planning, educators will neither make significant gains in the number of students adequately responding to core instruction nor ensure all students learn at the levels of depth and complexity necessary to graduate from high school ready for college or a skilled career.

Chapter 2: What Practices Make Up Tier 2 and Tier 3?

Planning a successful journey involves knowing the priorities of everyone on the trip, the budget that is available, and the time that can be allotted. Educators working to effect change in their schools also need to know who's with them and what skills those people have, and the money, time periods, and resources available to them. They must proactively address logistical questions related to school processes to ensure that the knowing-doing gap (the frustrating difference between knowing the shift that needs to occur and successfully implementing the shift) is closed.

This chapter addresses the following questions.

- Which students and student needs require more attention?
- Which staff members are best positioned to provide supports?

- When will these supports be provided in the school day?

- Where will these supports be provided?

- What resources, strategies, or programs are necessary to meet staff and student needs?

When schools address these questions, they are well on their way to establishing the critical structures of MTSS.

Chapter 3: Where Are We and What Are the Next Steps?

Every journey has a starting point, and to figure out where you need to go and to plan your journey, you need to know where you are right now. Before embarking on a new practice, it is important for educators to take a detailed look at what they are currently doing. A school's starting point can be established by using an evidence-based self-analysis of that school's current realities and state of readiness. This status report will reveal gaps and overlaps and initiate the collaborative approach necessary to refine or overhaul current practices.

Several factors must be taken into consideration at the start of any journey, including the mode of travel, the time required, and where the stops will be. As a school embarks on a process of change, it's important to think about questions such as, Where are we going? and Where are we now? Schools will strategically select next steps to address the areas of greatest need for staff and students.

A collaborative examination of the evidence from chapters 1 and 2 can help guide schools in their first steps or next steps. Several questions can guide this examination.

- In what areas do students need the most support?

- In what areas would staff members benefit from more support?

- Which initiatives would most significantly benefit students and most impact multiple content areas and domains?

- What initiatives are best prepared for, both in terms of culture and structures?

Chapter 4: What Stops Do We Make Along the Way?

To help avoid the ubiquitous question, Are we there yet?, the most successful trip planners build in the capacity to shift on the fly. They do this by allowing time in the schedule to spend an extra night at a favorite stop or to deal with flat tires. Successful school change requires similar check-ins and capacity to adjust to unforeseen difficulties and opportunities.

Just as students sometimes experience difficulties with executive functioning skills such as planning, organization, and time management, school teams can become stalled or sidetracked in their efforts. By following a systematic plan—one that prompts staff members to check on progress and anticipates pressure points—school leaders can ensure success. This ten-step plan is one that schools should follow to initiate, monitor, revise, and sustain MTSS-based school improvement. The plan makes a school's progress on the journey clear and provides the information needed for course corrections.

Chapter 5: What Does Student Evidence Reveal?

Evidence, provided through formal and informal assessments, is the engine that drives education. Evidence, when gathered accurately, analyzed collaboratively, and used to guide decisions, can motivate students and staff to expect more from themselves and to persevere through the difficulties that will arise. Schools have lots of data; however, data do not become evidence until educators make sense of the data in preparation for continuous improvement. Schools that maximize student outcomes through MTSS-based principles and practices thrive on evidence. Educators in such schools enthusiastically resolve the assessment paradox—that students are assessed too often and yet schools need more information about student needs.

Schools must gather the right evidence with the right tools.

- What evidence formats are necessary?
- Which students have significant gaps in the foundational prerequisite skills of literacy, numeracy, or behavior?
- To what extent are students learning the core content taught during initial, scaffolded, differentiated instruction?
- What antecedents, or reasons, explain the difficulties of students who are at risk of not mastering the desired learning outcomes?
- To what extent are students responding to supplemental supports?

When sites gather this information and take timely action, they are using evidence to drive their system of supports.

Appendix: Case Studies

As schools develop and implement the structures of MTSS, it is important to ensure that a culture exists in your school that supports high levels of learning for all students. The MTSS road map started by asking, "Where are we going?" Schools exist that are successfully serving students just like your school—schools in which the culture and the structures support continuous improvement and learning for adults and students.

Here, we provide examples to help schools with planning at this stage of the journey. Mature and successful school models such as those featured in the appendix show that it can be done. They inspire educators to energetically pursue the steps ahead and reveal where gaps between current realities and the desired destination may lie. Schools that are successfully implementing MTSS-based practices settle for nothing less than college and career readiness for all students.

Through the analysis of a mature MTSS model that serves as a guide and inspiration, schools can launch their efforts by responding to these questions.

- What is the school already doing?
- What is being done well?
- What are the gaps in supports for students?

Addressing these questions allows teams to leverage case studies to identify strengths and possible next steps in their system of supports.

The Journey Awaits

Significant shifts need to occur if schools are going to meet their lofty goals. Each school will have local, contextual needs that will require local, contextual responses. This will require educators to combine the principles of MTSS with new ways of thinking and applying research and proven practices to meet students' individual needs using the distinct talents and resources of the professionals who serve those students. The MTSS road map that follows will assist in determining a school's academic and behavioral system of supports for students and in designing localized, contextualized solutions and potential next steps. The journey awaits!

CHAPTER 1

What Practices and Elements Make Up Tier 1?

Any plans for a road trip begin with the premise that the trip is going to be fabulous (no one heads out with an intent to have a miserable time). The basic components foundational to the plan are locked in, such as type of transportation, hotels you'll be staying at, types of activities you'll be engaging in, and the types of meals you'll be consuming. These might be considered as universal (or Tier 1) expectations. We can similarly expect that the foundational aspects of instructional design and delivery are available to all. Schools engaged in deep, authentic MTSS practices have definitively answered the question, "What's the most important tier?" Tier 1, designed and defined through a process of prioritizing standards, unwrapping and unpacking those standards, and using the standards to drive both instruction and assessment, establishes the foundation for higher levels of student learning. A deep understanding of mapping, instruction, and assessment in academic and behavioral domains will ensure more students learn at deeper levels during core instructional blocks. Well-orchestrated mapping-instruction-assessment cycles will more accurately inform tiered, supplemental supports. A priority standards-driven and well-defined Tier 1 informs every aspect of MTSS.

Well-designed and intentional classroom instruction begins with a high-quality curriculum. Effective teachers do not simply teach such curriculum in a textbook-driven, page-by-page manner or in the same way for all students. Instead, they provide instruction designed to meet the specific needs of all students in the class, scaffolding, differentiating, and enriching based on evidence of student progress and learning. Tier 1 is driven by the strengths of the students in your current class—not last year's students, your best year's students, or the students you wish you had.

Schools that design and implement MTSS so that student outcomes improve share the following common features.

- All students who struggle academically or behaviorally receive high-quality instruction in general education settings. They are not placed in below-level courses or self-contained settings. When they require supplemental supports, they receive them *in addition to* core instruction, not *instead of* core instruction.

- All instruction is *evidence based* (we have evidence of student learning that validates that our practices are effective), is practically applied (we discuss our instructional delivery in terms of teaching methods), and can be validated as a best practice based on outcomes.

- All staff members (regular classroom teachers and other specialized teaching and support staff) work together in the planning and delivery of student instruction and in collecting and analyzing data about student performance.

- The teaching, learning, practice, and nurturing of behavioral skills are prioritized alongside core academics. Behavioral skills are explicitly taught in minilessons and reinforced throughout the day.

At Tier 1, these attributes provide the foundation for the work of everyone in a school. Typically, when school teams struggle to provide effective Tier 2 and Tier 3 supports, their problems can be traced back to neglect of some of the key components of a solid Tier 1 approach. For example, if a student continues to disrupt class and is sent to the office for the behavior, has that student been given clear Tier 1 instruction on what respect looks like? Has the teacher delivered explicit instruction that sounds like the following?

1. "Class, one of our key expectations is respect."

2. "One of the ways we demonstrate respect is by listening when someone is talking."

3. "If that person who is talking causes you to have an idea you'd like to share, the respectful thing to do is raise your hand."

4. "Here's what raising your hand looks like. All five fingers are up; there is no pumping of the arm or waving."

5. "Let's practice."

In this scenario, when there is a violation, the first recourse is to ensure (ask the student) if they know what respect looks like (tie it back to the expectation and the instruction) prior to any suggestion they need to be sent out or assigned to Tier 2 or Tier 3 help. If the number of students requiring Tier 2 and Tier 3 supports seems high, the problem likely resides in Tier 1 and not with having outliers.

Robert J. Marzano (2017) suggests all students deserve a guaranteed and viable curriculum. This ensures that all students have an equal opportunity to learn, as each student will have access to an effective or highly effective teacher and access to the same content, knowledge, and skills in each section or class. *Guaranteed* implies that every student is provided the opportunity to learn a core curriculum, providing them with a high probability of success in school. *Viable* suggests that schools make sure that the necessary time is available and protected so students will be able to learn the guaranteed curriculum. A guaranteed and viable curriculum is a key component of PLC culture as defined in *Learning by Doing* (DuFour, DuFour, Eaker, Many, & Mattos, 2016), and a PLC culture is a key component of MTSS.

Structure

Tiers are intended to define predictable supports that schools should proactively prepare to meet students' needs; support structures are classified in tiers, but students themselves are not labeled, defined, or tiered. See figure 1.1 (page 16).

Culture

We would like to reinforce a critical point—school culture matters (Lewis, Asberry, DeJarnett, & King, 2016). Governmental regulations, whether related to MTSS or any other initiative, rarely mention the importance of culture. However, we are certain that six months into any new effort, the difficulties that schools face will relate more to the culture of the school than to the structures that have been established. Consider this: "Culture shared by all school stakeholders makes the actualization of both short- and long-term objectives easier" (Lewis et al., 2016, p. 57).

What do we mean by culture? A positive school culture has the following characteristics.

- It is rich in trust and respect.
- There is recognition that collaborative processes are fundamental, that there is a collective commitment to affecting the changes that will produce positive outcomes.

Tier 1 Engaging, differentiated instruction for all students
☐ Consists of a guaranteed and viable curriculum that will result in mastery (not just coverage) of essentials to the level of depth and complexity required to be future ready.
☐ Features differentiated and scaffolded pedagogies, strategies, and routines so that all students can access core content and engage meaningfully in their zones of proximal development.
☐ This guaranteed, viable curriculum addresses both academic and behavioral domains.
Tier 2 More time and differentiated supports for students who have not mastered the essentials, as measured by regular assessments designed to inform instruction
☐ Supports for students who require more time and alternative strategies and approaches to master the content initially addressed in Tier 1.
☐ Involves gathering evidence about which students will require support and with which skills, behavioral attributes, and academic learning targets they will need alternative strategies and approaches, as well as securing the time, personnel, and resources to respond.
☐ Is validated by researchers, including Benjamin Bloom (1968, 1974, 1984), who demonstrated that an impressive 95 percent of students will achieve mastery of essential content with these Tier 2 supports as a companion to Tier 1 instruction, a model he named *mastery learning*.
☐ Tier 2 supports (more time and alternative strategies and approaches to master Tier 1 essentials) can be applied to behavioral as well as academic learning targets.
Tier 3 For students who have been screened to be multiple grade levels behind their peers in foundational skills (and for students who have not responded to Tier 1 and Tier 2 supports)
☐ Supports students who experience significant difficulties with any and all content because of deficits in their foundational literacy, numeracy, and behavior skills.
☐ Requires that we identify students and their areas of deficit early; identification need not be laborious; the process is typically known as universal screening.
☐ Involves providing intensive, targeted supports to begin closing gaps with a great sense of urgency; for example, each school year must end with educators having a solid understanding of students requiring Tier 3 supports, and an emerging understanding of the antecedents of their struggles, so that the next year's intensive interventions can begin the first week of school.

Figure 1.1: Criteria for successful tiered supports.

*Visit **go.SolutionTree.com/schoolimprovement** for a free reproducible version of this figure.*

- New initiatives are not repeatedly and haphazardly begun. Instead, depth (of student learning and of staff priorities) is valued over breadth.

- All students are valued and expected to make significant gains in their learning. Factors that may inhibit gains are viewed as temporary obstacles and challenges that will eventually be successfully overcome.

- All staff members accept responsibility for all students: students in other classrooms, students in other grade levels, students with different sexual orientations or race, students with disabilities, and students who speak another language at home.

- The status quo is never accepted; as expectations for students are appropriately raised, staff members recognize continuous improvement as the habit of great organizations. When areas for improvement are identified, change is accepted as an opportunity and all variables are considered.

- The prevalent attitude is, "We'll do whatever it takes." Educators view adult behaviors as having the most effective and significant influence on student learning and behaviors.

We have observed practices in schools, districts, and divisions that have *not* led to positive cultures. Here are some lessons we can convey.

- **Death-by-initiative is a condition plaguing many school systems and organizations:** A new idea or program every year, or seven new initiatives in a single year, is bound to leave staff feeling overwhelmed and certain to guarantee that no idea is optimally employed on behalf of students. We understand the dilemma—there are many areas that need our attention, and there are many ideas and practices that would potentially benefit staff and students. We must, however, resist the temptation to introduce too much at one time. We must accept the likelihood that a single, wisely chosen initiative in one area of schooling can actually impact many of the areas in which students need support.

- **Top-down decisions never result in sustainable change:** While we believe strongly in the value of good leadership and in leaders leading, all educators agree that a balance of centralized (to organize, to guide, to facilitate communication) and decentralized (to provide input, to shape the actual products, to refine the work) decision making is the wisest, most respectful, and most productive way in which any powerful system should be initiated. When decisions are made by fiat, from central offices or school offices, without meaningful input from stakeholders, MTSS often fails to reach its full potential. A collaborative approach to designing and implementing a system of supports for all students will more likely result in support from both principals and staff members; while this is critical, this approach involves much more. School-based staff members can identify what's working well, can accurately report current realities and states of readiness, and can report on areas where professional development is most needed.

- **Leading change takes time:** In our professional experience, we find that planning for MTSS-based practices months or even a year in advance leads to the deepest, most successful, most sustained change. We advocate the notion of a three- to five-year commitment to this work (depending on your starting point) and remind colleagues that if it could happen in three to five weeks or months, then it should already be in place. Effective practice takes time. *Ineffective* practice takes even more time.

- **Staff members must receive initial and ongoing supports on MTSS-based endeavors:** We have observed many willing educators who struggle with tasks, such as organizing their collaborative problem solving, determining student needs, or monitoring progress, because they did not receive an appropriate quality and quantity of professional development. Human, fiscal, and temporal resources must be budgeted to support educators in initiating and sustaining MTSS.

- **Cover a realistic number of standards:** We must ensure that students master only those standards that we have identified as the highest priority. For example, we worry that schools often misdiagnose students as having a learning disability simply because educators have attempted to cover an unreasonable number of standards in a short period of time. Not all standards are equally important—and in any case, while standards are important for defining the content, we are not teaching students *standards*—we are teaching students to *solve problems and think critically.* Some students may require more prerequisite supports; some may require more time to master the most highly prioritized standards; all students will benefit from more opportunities to learn the most highly prioritized standards to greater levels of depth and complexity.

- **Educators increasingly accept responsibility for explicitly addressing students' behaviors:** Behavior-focused learning includes those skills in the domains of mindsets, social skills, perseverance, learning strategies, and academic behaviors described in this book. If we commit to providing students with explicit instruction in behaviors (and we must), then we must plan for greater focus of the academic content to make time for this critical behavior instruction.

- **Interventions that are not provided systemically—not only in isolated classrooms—will not fully realize the potential of MTSS:** The system must be built on, and powered by, collaborative teams, and collaborative teams will most powerfully meet student needs by implementing the practices of MTSS. Collaborative cultures—between teams of teachers, teachers and administrators, clinicians and teachers, general and special education, grade levels, and content areas—are a prerequisite for successfully implementing MTSS. Have a plan for how important information is shared. Establish expectations and norms. Keep it simple but remember to communicate.

- **There is no MTSS without monitoring:** We must determine the extent to which students are responding. Insufficient monitoring compromises the success of MTSS, both for an individual student and for a school. School leaders must identify who will take the lead on monitoring, how frequently monitoring will occur, what tools will be used, and how results will be utilized. Results can motivate students and educators; they can inform adjustments to supports needed to make an individual student successful; and they can validate the success of interventions or suggest that for too many students, interventions are not resulting in success. Data, information, and evidence make up the engine that drives MTSS.

We are fortunate enough to work at, and with, exceptional schools, school districts, and school divisions, and we have observed practices in schools, districts, and divisions that have greatly contributed to positive cultures.

Best practices in the area of culture are best illustrated by the following.

- **Schools and school leaders who have successfully led MTSS-based initiatives have demonstrated a respect for change:** Change creates anxiety because we fear failure, a loss of control, lack of support, personal impact, and the unknown. Knowing the potential resistance to change by some, and the reasons why change might be resisted, school leaders must do the following.

  → Describe the why and what of change.

  → Present research on, and rationale for, the change.

  → Provide time for stakeholders to reflect on the change.

  → Provide staff members with the opportunity to voice opinions.

  → Describe the professional learning for the new endeavor that will be provided and the ways in which the effectiveness of the new endeavor will be measured.

  → Determine whether consensus for the change exists, moving forward only once consensus is achieved.

  → Hold one another accountable for implementing the change through regular progress checks and supports if needed.

- **Like all initiatives, MTSS must be implemented with transparency and trust:** There is no such thing as too much communication. Leaders must continually and repeatedly describe the following.

  → Why the change is necessary

  → What is expected (and what is not expected)

  → How successfully the change is progressing

Some stakeholders will have concerns and questions during the implementation. Site, district, and division leaders should schedule frequent times during which staff members can voice their concerns and questions and during which leaders listen. Leadership and change require courage. Proposing change requires courage. Initiating the change requires courage. Holding colleagues accountable for change requires courage. Making modifications to the change requires courage.

Core Content

MTSS can perhaps best be understood through the lens of educator actions. We believe that the most critical initial and ongoing tasks of teacher teams are prioritizing, unpacking, and unwrapping standards; employing effective instructional strategies; designing flexible units; and proactively and courageously addressing the culture of the school. These tasks are fundamental to MTSS and to ensuring that all students—whether students with lower current levels of readiness, students on grade level, or students with more well-developed current levels of readiness—respond to initial instruction.

Instructional design and delivery start with carefully and completely defining key core content. The need to do this is driven by the following considerations.

- The curriculum is only guaranteed and viable if students in a grade or course learn the same core content or skills (standards) no matter what teacher they have (making it guaranteed) *and* a team of educators clearly defines a reasonable quantity of content for all students to learn in the available time (making it viable; Marzano, 2017).

- We need to ensure a guaranteed and viable curriculum by teaching all standards, but not as if they are all equally important (Marzano, 2017). There are too many standards (DuFour & Marzano, 2011; Schmoker, 2012), and if we do not prioritize standards, we risk favoring quantity over quality and breadth over depth. While not all students may master some lower-priority standards, all students must master the essential standards.

- Standards must be unpacked so that educators and students know what mastery looks like, so that instruction can match these expectations, and so that teams of educators can plan backward from assessments that measure these expectations (McTighe & Wiggins, 2012).

- The better our understanding of content and the more precisely we unpack standards, the better our assessments of student learning will be. This leads to more accurate identifications of students in need of extra support, more diagnostic analyses of specific areas of need, and more targeted interventions.

- We cannot intervene and provide more time and differentiated supports on all standards with students who are at risk of dropping out; identifying the essential learning (prioritized standards) helps determine the focus of interventions.

Standards

To achieve the desired outcomes, schools and school districts need to plan for the following key steps (all of which collaborative teams drive).

These three steps are prerequisites and fundamental to our MTSS efforts at all tiers.

1. **Prioritize which standards or learning targets are the most critical for all students to master.** We will use prioritized standards synonymously with essential, power, need-to-know, or critical standards. We *prioritize* standards to guarantee the viability of our curriculum.

2. **Unpack standards so all teachers and students understand the level of rigor and format associated with mastery, as well as the types of learning that logically precede and follow mastery of the essentials.** We *unpack* standards to inform a consistently understood depth of instruction from which we can plan backward.

3. **Unwrap standards to ensure that we are assessing student mastery as accurately and authentically as possible.** For example, not all learning can be assessed with a multiple-response test. We will misidentify students in need of extra assistance and miss opportunities to learn about the effectiveness of instruction if we do not more accurately match assessments to the levels of understanding that we expect. We *unwrap* standards to inform the ways in which we assess students and to determine the instruction that will prepare them for the task.

Each of these is essential to defining key core content, so we examine each one in further detail.

The work of prioritizing, unpacking, and unwrapping standards will positively impact student learning when it is done collaboratively by teacher teams with the support of principals, district and site content area coaches, and district office personnel. Let's be clear: this work takes time, effort, cooperation, and compromise. Start by building the shared decision that this is the right, first task when implementing MTSS. The logical place to begin is with the core Tier 1 delivery.

Prioritizing Standards

Standards represent a broad set of learning targets for students to master at an appropriate level of depth and complexity. This broad nature of standards often makes identifying levels of performance difficult when looking at the entirety of the standard. Therefore, teams of teachers must prioritize. While there may be five standards represented in a unit of study, teams must identify which are need-to-know and which are nice-to-know. Not unexpectedly, this process is difficult for teams who are intimate with the content. One team of teachers that can definitely assist in defining the essential grade-level content for students to master is next year's teachers, who will assume primary responsibility for those students' learning in a year's time. In other words, if third-grade teachers are struggling to discern between need-to-know and nice-to-know, they should talk with their fourth-grade colleagues. Evidence of student learning and vertical articulation between grade levels and adjacent courses will lead to more informed decisions on the most critical content for students to master.

When core Tier 1 instruction focuses on depth over breadth, all students benefit. Those students with lower levels of readiness will have time to receive preteaching and reteaching in the unit of instruction. Those students currently at grade level engage with prioritized content at more depth and complexity. They get time to practice and deepen their understanding. Those students with more well-developed levels of readiness will have time to explore enriched aspects of the prioritized standards. They get the opportunity to enrich their skills in extensions of the content rather than getting more of the same content. More students respond to initial instruction. This applies to academic skills, just as it applies to behaviors.

Educators should examine, or re-examine, content in light of MTSS by asking themselves the following questions.

- **Is it possible that a large percentage of students are deemed at risk simply because of the overwhelming quantity of content standards that we have attempted to teach and that they have attempted to learn?** Research repeatedly shows that the performance of U.S. students is average, and often below average, when compared to other industrialized nations (DeSilva, 2017). This remains true even when comparing the United States' highest-performing states and most affluent students. A typical U.S. fourth-grade mathematics text totals 530 pages; a typical international fourth-grade mathematics text totals 170 pages. A typical *U.S.* fourth-grade science text totals 397 pages; a typical *international* fourth-grade science text totals 125 pages. The

United States averages seventy-eight mathematics topics in a school, while Germany averages twenty-three and Japan seventeen. Students from both Germany and Japan significantly outperform U.S. students. While other differences between teaching and learning between the United States and higher-performing nations are a consideration, the sheer number of U.S. standards is undeniably vast and impacts these results.

- **Can we guarantee that those students who are currently meeting proficiency standards are on track to graduate ready for college or a skilled career?** A Northwest Evaluation Association (NWEA) analysis of tens of thousands of students nationwide finds that students who met the adequate yearly performance benchmark on one large state's No Child Left Behind Act of 2001 examination nevertheless scored at the 20th percentile on NWEA assessments (Cronin & Jensen, 2014; Cronin, Kingsbury, Dahlin, & Bowe, 2007). A potential crisis may exist because a *separate* NWEA study (Cronin et al., 2007) correlates college and career readiness closer to the 65th percentile, suggesting that NWEA's own evaluations may misrepresent students' academic status. We may be communicating to teachers, students, and families that all is well when, in fact, there exists a large gap between meeting state and federal expectations and college and career readiness.

It may be fair to conclude that we must help students go deeper and solve more complex tasks. It's unlikely that any teacher would suggest that this is possible with the current number of standards. We must focus.

Unpacking Standards

Teams unpack standards so that they build collective consensus on what it looks like when students meet grade-level standards. Learning targets help make greater sense of standards for both staff and students. Teachers are clear on what learning does and does not look like, and they design their instruction to meet these outcomes. In addition, unpacking standards informs differentiation. When teams describe in detail the quality of student work that will be required to demonstrate mastery of standards, they are in a great position to identify both necessary prerequisites and appropriate extensions.

Finally, unpacking standards ensures that teachers and students are crystal clear regarding the expectations of the prioritized standards. These unpacked standards drive instruction in a unit. Ideally, unpacking standards should lead to fewer students experiencing difficulty, since coverage of a breadth of all standards is rejected in favor of a depth of mastery of prioritized standards. A thorough unpacking of standards also informs Tier 2 supports in a system of MTSS; when the full meaning of a standard is understood, both students and teachers can better determine which aspects have been learned and which have not yet been learned.

Unwrapping Standards

It should be clear by now that standards, instruction, and assessment continuously interact. It's often unclear where one ends and the other begins—and this is OK. As an example, the need to devote more time to prerequisite standards is made clear when frequent, formative checks for understanding reveal gaps in students' prior knowledge.

The unpacking process produces learning targets that drive instruction. The unwrapping process produces *success criteria*, which illustrate what mastery of learning targets looks and sounds like. Success criteria inform assessment design and ensure that assessment items accurately measure the standards and targets that were taught in a unit.

Behavior Needs

Educational psychologists agree there are five domains of behavior (Farrington et al., 2012): (1) mindsets, (2) social skills, (3) perseverance, (4) learning strategies, and (5) academic behaviors. Behavior and academics are inextricably linked. This is particularly true for students at risk (Buffum et al., 2012; Hierck et al., 2011; Weber, 2018). When students are not responding to core instruction in essential academic content, the causes of these difficulties may be deficits in basic academic needs—students may have deficits in reading, writing, or number sense that are compromising their ability to access content or demonstrate mastery. Alternatively, students who are not responding to core instruction in essential academic content may simply need more time or differentiated supports.

Another possibility we must consider is that a student's behavior, in either the domain of social or academic behaviors (such as self-regulatory strategies or executive functioning skills), is inhibiting success in mastering grade-level or content essentials. It is rare to find a student whose academic difficulties have not led to behavioral challenges (National Center for Learning Disabilities, 2017), and it is equally rare to find a student whose not-yet-developed behaviors do not significantly impede learning (Duckworth, Taxer, Eskreis-Winkler, Galla, & Gross, 2019). As mentioned previously, we must accept responsibility for teaching students the behaviors that we want to see. It comes down to this simple notion: If you haven't taught it, why are you expecting to see it? In our MTSS approach, this must be true for all the outcomes we expect our students to achieve—academically or behaviorally.

We urge you to make the same commitment to behaviors as to academics and to apply the same curricular, instructional, and assessment practices to behavior as to academics. This starts with prioritizing the behaviors (from the behavioral skills in the five domains) that align with your student and school needs. For example, unpacking prioritized standards does not simply ensure that teachers and students understand the rigor and format associated with mastery; it also prepares teams of teachers to respond when students do not initially learn or when students demonstrate mastery shortly after beginning a unit. We must unpack behavioral skills just as we unpack academic skills. See the book *Behavior: The Forgotten Curriculum* (Weber, 2018) for an in-depth discussion.

SEL

Educators are likely familiar with the five competencies of social-emotional learning (SEL; Collaborative for Academic, Social, and Emotional Learning [CASEL], 2020). They align and intersect very well with the five domains of behavior or noncognitive factors (Farrington et al., 2012) referenced throughout this book. As a reminder, here are the five competencies with a brief description.

1. **Self-awareness:** Recognition of one's own emotions, personal goals, and values

2. **Self-management:** Regulation of one's own emotions and behaviors

3. **Social awareness:** Understanding of and compassion for others' backgrounds or cultures

4. **Relationship skills:** Ability to establish and maintain healthy relationships

5. **Responsible decision making:** Making positive choices involving one's own behavior

Implementing SEL in the classroom should be aligned with a school's positive behavior supports and in alignment with the five domains of behavior. Along with trauma-informed and social justice practices (page 29), they make up a school's Tier 1 behavioral curriculum.

Teachers can further the work by considering these four steps.

1. Define goals for your school, including behavior expectations.

2. Spell out what those goals and expectations look like not only in your classroom but also in any other areas your students may interact with (the gymnasium, library, lunchroom, hallways, bathrooms, and bus lines, for example).

3. Develop your skills to teach behavioral skills through professional learning. Model the skills as an extension of the instruction.

4. Model, teach, nurture, and practice SEL and other behavioral skills.

Here's an example of Tier 1 instruction that could occur for each of the SEL components. These examples also address the noncognitive factors.

- **Self-awareness:** Start a lesson by checking in on students' emotions. This could be as simple as asking, "How is your motor running today?" Students can respond with thumbs-up for too fast (angry or anxious), too slow (sad or overtired), or just right (content or happy), and discuss why. Referencing how that affects behavior and decision making provides the connection needed to deepen this component.

- **Self-management:** Help students to set goals and define steps to achieve those goals as a way to manage their own learning. It may be a learning target tracker or a simpler agenda that they use to manage their time to complete assignments. Developing self-management also means providing further instruction (not consequences in isolation) when goals are not met.

- **Social awareness:** Teachers assist students in practicing social awareness and the ability to empathize with others by identifying and acknowledging that there are various ways to approach a problem. Highlighting multiple ways to solve a mathematics problem and having students explain their strategy builds this key skill.

- **Relationship skills:** When students are purposefully grouped for instructional strategies, they have the opportunity to work on their relationship skills. Teachers support students in developing these skills early and often through ice-breaker activities that build community. Reflecting on what makes a good group or what each member contributes to the group reinforces the notion that relationship skills are important. Modeling, teaching, nurturing, and practicing social skills, one of the five noncognitive factor domains described in the appendix (page 115), can help students develop these social-emotional skills.

- **Responsible decision making:** Students tend to both follow and respect the expectations for classroom learning when they understand how expectations are aligned and when they co-construct those expectations. Working collectively and engaging in responsible decision making to achieve consensus reinforces awareness of the impact of their personal decision-making process. Restorative practices also help with responsible decision making, empowering and requiring students to monitor their behavior.

Developing the five component skills of SEL as part of Tier 1 instruction also starts the process of identifying students who struggle with these foundational skills and will inform Tier 2 and 3 supports.

Key Lenses

As teachers provide Tier 1 lessons, they must also be prepared for their core instruction to evolve as science and culture evolve. The following sections look at instructional design as it relates to equity, trauma, and social justice.

Equity

We discuss equity as focusing on meeting the needs of a socioeconomically, culturally, and linguistically diverse student population. *Equity* often gets confused with *equality* as issues of fairness get framed around every student getting the same things (equality) instead of the things they need (equity).

Historically, equitable instructional practices always needed to be differentiated, scaffolded, inclusive, and engaging; that need has become even clearer. In addition, it must respectively meet the affective needs of all learners.

Focusing on equity in the classroom involves considering the following when designing your lessons and delivering instruction.

- **Recognizing that students experience curriculum differently and building on their unique experiences to make the curriculum more accessible:** Context matters in making curriculum attainable. Having an Inuit student in Nunavut (a region near the Arctic Circle) solve a mathematics problem involving 72 kumquats lacks context or relevance for the student, who may never have even seen a kumquat. It does not get to the core of mathematics knowledge.

- **Creating multiple options for knowledge acquisition and demonstration:** Not every student is proficient on first instruction, despite brilliant lesson design and delivery. Having many ways to share content and many options to demonstrate knowledge acquisition allows for sense making to occur.

- **Providing different work, not more of the same:** Volume is not enrichment; it's poor planning. Are there other routes to demonstrating learning both at acquiring proficiency and at moving beyond proficiency?

Scholar and author Yvette Jackson suggests, "Cultural responsiveness is not a practice; it's what informs our practice so that we can make better teaching choices for eliciting, engaging, motivating, supporting, and expanding the intellectual capacity of ALL our students" (as cited in Hammond, 2015, p. vii; capitalization in original). This distinction between *being* a practice and *informing* a practice is key.

Educators and schools should consider addressing issues of equity with the following actions.

- Teachers can ensure that students of all backgrounds receive equitable instruction by acknowledging students' cultural heritage and accommodating multiple modes of learning.

- Schools can create welcoming environments for diverse families by showcasing student diversity and offering parent education activities.

- Schools can engage hard-to-reach families by communicating in their home language, meeting them in their own communities, and taking steps to make family participation easier.

Schools should discuss questions like those in figure 1.2 (page 30) to address these efforts.

Trauma

Kathleen Fitzgerald Rice and Betsy McAlister Groves (2005, p. 3, as cited by Souers & Hall, 2016, p. 15) define trauma as "an exceptional experience in which powerful and dangerous events overwhelm a person's capacity to cope." Understanding the significance of this definition and the impact is critical as we strive to serve all students and student needs and ensure that all students master essential behavioral and academic outcomes; trauma significantly impacts an individual's abilities to master either. Trauma does not occur evenly or equitably (as the COVID-19 pandemic revealed). Every teacher is likely working with students who have experienced, or are experiencing, trauma.

How do educators best support students with diverse needs?
What can leadership do to provide training on culturally responsive teaching practices?
What languages make up your school population?
Can parents access information in their familiar language? Are there faculty members, community volunteers, or organizations who can assist?
What can school and district leadership do to engage diverse families?
What are you doing to welcome all families to your classroom?
Can you link families who speak the same language?
What can school and district leadership do to ensure participation in school events for culturally and linguistically diverse families?

Source: Adapted from Hanover Research, 2017.

Figure 1.2: Equity-addressing questions.

*Visit **go.SolutionTree.com/schoolimprovement** for a free reproducible version of this figure.*

John Eller and Tom Hierck (2021), in *Trauma-Sensitive Instruction: Creating a Safe and Predictable Classroom Environment*, describe a *trauma-sensitive learning environment* as one "designed by the teacher to minimize its impact on continuing or extending traumatic situations for students" (pp. 53–54). We encourage teachers to regularly examine both the structure and procedures they use in their classrooms to ensure that the environment is trauma sensitive. This process may well be more complex at the start of a year or term but will be easier as you get to know your students.

Equally important in the examination of student needs is to imagine the impact of classroom practices and procedures from a student perspective. If the practice or procedure is not essential to the safe operation of your classroom, why is it important to maintain, particularly if that practice or procedure triggers an undesirable student reaction or behavior? Operating your classroom using predictable, essential practices and procedures can help eliminate unnecessary disruption and reactions for students.

All teachers should consider completing an assessment of their learning environment, looking for areas that might be contributing to trauma or adding to outside traumatic situations. The reproducible "Identifying and Changing Potential Learning Environment Problem Areas" (page 35) helps educators identify potential problem areas and make necessary adjustments to design classroom learning environments that are more trauma sensitive.

Social Justice

Social justice is about more than the protection of rights but encompasses reinforcing the need for all people to participate fully in civic life. The aim, then, of social justice is to achieve a just and equitable society. It involves recognizing and acting on the power that each of us has for making positive change. The reality is that teachers do this every day in many ways. Formalizing the practice ensures it becomes part of how all classrooms operate daily and not simply an occasional practice in isolated situations.

As with all the other instructional practices described in this chapter, the strategies in this section align well with what any educator would describe as best practices of teaching. In other words, this is not an add-on but an aligned practice deeply connected to producing successful students. As professor of education Tabitha Dell'Angelo (2014) says:

> This isn't something that just gets done in diverse classrooms, or classrooms that lack diversity, or urban classrooms—or any other special category of school. It is a way of teaching and being that supports high-level thinking and learning throughout our lives.

Dell'Angelo (2014) goes on to suggest some key strategies summarized in the following sections.

- Connecting to students' lives
- Linking to real-world problems and multiple perspectives
- Creating classroom communities

Connecting to Students' Lives

Consider, value, and build on the diverse prior learning experiences of your students. This can be as simple as knowing a little bit about every student's background. Hierck (2017) suggests teachers should learn every student's DNA—not what might have been instructed in science class—but instead defined as their *dreams*, *needs*, and *abilities*. By acknowledging what students are already bringing to the classroom, teachers take an important step toward creating a classroom for social justice.

Linking to Real-World Problems and Multiple Perspectives

Make what you are teaching relevant to what is going on in the world. If there is something happening in the news that you can link to your content, spend a reasonable amount of class time addressing this real-world situation. Ask students if they have questions regarding anything they have been hearing about. This is an opportunity to teach students high-level thinking skills such as discerning fact from opinion and figuring out your own and others' point of view.

Creating Classroom Communities

Create opportunities for students' voices to be heard and teach them how to participate in a discussion. The teacher's role is to use questioning that can help students make connections between the big ideas that inform the lesson content. Examine your course materials to ensure that your materials include examples from diverse aspects of society, including ethnicity, religion, language, gender, ability, sexual orientation, and socioeconomic status in a non-stereotypical manner.

With all the included strategies, teachers have many ways to advocate for their inclusion in core Tier 1 instruction. The most important initial step may be to model the expectations you want to see in your classroom. Try to find ways to include some of the ideas outlined with the practices that you know have worked best for you and your students.

Standards-Based Grading

In a traditional grading approach, students' overall grades are determined by combining academic and nonacademic components, such as classwork, participation, attendance, and homework with academic measures such as quizzes and exams. Each component has a weight assigned to influence the final grade accordingly. By contrast, in a standards-based approach, nonacademic components (such as attendance, effort, and homework) are not included in the final grade. Also, standards-based grading aggregates all student work on one standard to determine if students have achieved mastery or need to improve their knowledge in one area.

In the absence of first establishing a standards-based mindset, educators may well remain entrenched in traditional grading thought processes—using tactics that include applying penalties, assigning zeroes, grading everything, and averaging results earned by students. We need a new paradigm that focuses on assessment as an evidence chase and not a number chase, from viewing grades as a reward bestowed by the teacher to grades that reflect the learning students have achieved. As Tom Schimmer (2016) suggests:

> It only makes sense that teaching to standards means reporting on those very same standards. If the information we collect and report is free of any nonstandard-related distortions (such as effort, penalties, completion scores, and attitude), we can create a mutually supportive relationship and establish a seamless formative-summative experience for students, parents, and teachers. (p. 15)

Recognize that core Tier 1 instruction has high-quality evidence as its engine, to validate both instructional design and delivery. To provide the clearest picture of student learning related to the desired outcomes (the standards), educators must have that evidence be as clean and pristine in relation to learning as possible. Teachers cannot gather evidence that is free of the variety of identified biases if schools stick with the traditional paradigm of grades and grading.

Standards-based grading is a game-changer in MTSS. In fact, one might argue that MTSS cannot fully be implemented in the absence of standards-based principles and practices. There are several guides to standards-based grading, including *A School Leader's Guide to Standards-Based Grading* (Heflebower, Hoegh, & Warrick, 2014) and *Planning and Teaching in the Standards-Based Classroom* (Flygare, Hoegh, & Heflebower, 2022). For our purposes, we strive to use assessment, grading, and feedback practices that increase hope, efficacy, achievement, and accuracy through standards-based grading.

Here are six key elements of standards-based grading to consider.

1. Clear learning targets and success criteria

2. Assessments aligned to learning targets

3. Formative assessments that provide feedback to students and teachers prior to the summative

4. Feedback and grades that are aligned to learning targets and reported in proficiency levels, not percentages

5. Opportunities to demonstrate growth in understanding through reassessment after reteaching and relearning

6. Grades that authentically reflect what students know, not how they got there

Standards-based grading is a vital component of a school's practices and a critical element of MTSS.

Summary

The cultures and structures associated with schools' MTSS-based practices will continuously require leaders' and educators' attention. While school culture—the beliefs and attitudes of staff members—provides the foundation that prepares for and sustains the work, structures are also critical components. Ensuring that the structures of MTSS practices are systematically and successfully in place requires that school leaders and educators address key questions. Although it requires knowledge and persistence, answering these questions is well in our capacity as professional educators. Asking the questions in a proactive and committed manner is the key to success.

Identifying and Changing Potential Learning Environment Problem Areas

List the suspected trauma areas that may be impacting your students.

List the processes or procedures in your learning environment that seem to trigger undesirable behaviors.

List the evidence that makes you think these processes or procedures are triggering problems.

Implement changes in processes or procedures that you think would help make your learning environment more trauma sensitive.

What is your timeline for making these changes in your classroom? What resources will you need in order to make these changes?

Source: Eller, J., & Hierck, T. (2021). Trauma-sensitive instruction: Creating a safe and predictable classroom environment. *Bloomington, IN: Solution Tree Press.*

CHAPTER 2

What Practices Make Up
Tier 2 and Tier 3?

Planning a successful journey involves knowing the priorities of everyone on the trip, the budget that is available, and the time that can be allotted. Although the people on the journey may have experience with travel from taking previous road trips, it's easy to contemplate that something on the trip may require skills beyond the expertise of those on the journey. If an indicator on your car lights up, you and your traveling companions may not possess the expertise to address the need. It may be as easy as an oil change or as complex as a blown head gasket. This will be the time to turn to an expert who can identify and remedy the problem quickly and effectively to allow the journey to proceed.

Educators looking to effect change in their schools also need to know who's with them and what skills those people have, and the money, time periods, and resources they have at their disposal. As they contemplate the need for Tier 2 and Tier 3 interventions, they do so with an aim toward having additional expertise brought into the conversation and planning. These phases of the MTSS road map prepare us, as educators, for the final stage of the journey, because there are students in our schools for whom differentiated core instruction will not be enough to ensure high levels of access and achievement.

To foster the construction of a system of supports, educators must ask, "What are the critical structures of an MTSS model?" They must proactively address logistical questions related to school processes.

- Which students and student needs require more attention?
- Which staff members are best positioned to provide supports?
- When will these supports be provided in the school day?

- Where will these supports be provided?

- What resources, strategies, or programs are necessary to meet needs?

- To what extent are students responding to supports?

The school's initial answers to these questions may change as they get more or new evidence, and they must be prepared to include the third critical element of MTSS: problem solving to determine the appropriate course of action.

When and Where to Provide Supports During the School Day

Time is our most precious resource. Because we know that supplemental supports will best be provided during the regular school day, when students are obligated to attend school and all staff are working within their contractual day, and because we would rather not remove students from core Tier 1 instruction to provide supports, the challenge of when to provide MTSS-based interventions can paralyze implementation teams. The following sections examine when to provide Tier 2 and 3 supports.

When and Where to Provide Tier 2 Interventions

We recommend that schools strongly consider embedding a thirty-minute intervention block daily—or four days per week, given that many schools have an alternative schedule one day per week to provide time for staff collaboration. As often happens in education, the word *intervention* has become negatively associated and suggestive of time devoted only to the "struggling students or red-zone kids." This unfortunate, and actually incorrect, stereotype of the term *intervention* adds another layer of challenge when educators discuss making time for this important block. These blocks of time allow for differentiated Tier 2 supports for all students, in addition to those provided during Tier 1 blocks of instruction. Students who need more time and alternative supports to master essential content can receive that Tier 2 support during the thirty-minute block without missing instruction in any other content. Students ready to go deeper and engage in problems and tasks of greater complexity can do so during the same block.

When scheduled carefully, staff members can be freed to meet student needs during these time periods, potentially resulting in lower-than-normal class sizes. A fresh set of eyes is often helpful to examine schedules, challenge the status quo, and examine inefficiencies that may exist. Ability grouping often emerges during these discussions. We feel that a balanced approach is best, a viewpoint validated by the balance of research (Hattie, 2009). During core Tier 1 blocks of instruction, we recommend that students be grouped heterogeneously (recognizing that students are likely to meet with the teacher in small groups based on student readiness). During Tier 2 blocks of instruction, such as the thirty-minute block described here, students can be grouped more homogeneously based on need, with groupings revised as new evidence reveals the need for more time and alternative approaches for students to master a new set of essentials. We would also suggest during this block that schools adopt an all-hands-on-deck approach that sees every adult in the building assigned a group of students with which to work. This provides the opportunity to keep groups smaller (particularly those students identified as *not yet* in terms of proficiency on essential learning targets) and match the skills of the adults with the needs of the students.

When and Where to Provide Tier 3 Interventions

While well-designed and well-delivered Tier 1 and Tier 2 supports meet the needs of many students—Bloom's (1968, 1984) landmark research places the percentage at 95 percent—we will still have students who require intensive supports. Just as we can predict that some students will require a little more time and a different approach to master essentials, we can predict that some students will require even more support to get on track to graduate ready for college or a skilled career. These students typically have significant deficits in foundational skills and will require timely, targeted, and intensive Tier 3 intervention. The dilemma is when to provide them.

Consider these assertions (Buffum, Mattos, Weber, & Hierck, 2015).

- Students multiple grade levels behind their peers will not catch up in the absence of immediate, intensive, targeted supports.

- Students multiple grade levels behind their peers will likely fail classes, experience frustration, and may not graduate from high school at all or may not graduate ready for college or a skilled career in the absence of immediate, intensive, targeted supports.

- Students losing access to core literacy and mathematics instruction risk falling behind in grade-level essentials as they learn skills from prior grade levels.

The courage to accept responsibility for all students learning at high levels is based on the following.

- The deeply held belief that all students can learn.

- The recognition that literacy, numeracy, and behavior are fundamental skills that can and should be prioritized.

- A commitment to the arts and sciences for all students, in conjunction with a commitment to build literacy and numeracy when illiteracy and innumeracy exist.

Students who are identified through screening and assessment to have significant foundational deficits, and for whom intensive Tier 3 supports are deemed necessary and appropriate, must also have access to Tier 1 and 2 supports. Schools increasingly embracing this practice are designing schedules that include Tier 2 blocks of time for all students. When, though, can intensive Tier 3 supports be scheduled? These supports might need to be provided—temporarily, reluctantly, and flexibly—in place of other equally important course content. In the case studies in the appendix (page 115), these intensive supports were sometimes provided in place of science, social studies, or electives on a rotating basis.

We recommend that schools discuss this issue openly and discuss the priority they place on content areas and skills in the school. It is important to relay that this is not a judgment on the value of individual staff members. Teachers of physical education, art, science, and social studies are teachers of children first, and children who lack literacy and numeracy skills are ill prepared for later grade levels and for life (Centers for Disease Control and Prevention, 2022). The reproducible "Prioritize Content" (page 46) can help educators determine the priority of various content areas.

Students who desperately need intensive, targeted Tier 3 supports—supports for which designated times are unlikely to exist—may need to miss another content area, but *they need not always miss the same content area*, and *they need not miss all the content*. There should not be a universal decision made that all students could miss the same, designated course (often an elective) as the first step toward scheduling Tier 3. As circumstances permit, the decision should be made on an individual student basis. Examples follow.

- Elementary and secondary schools may vary the time or the period during which intensive supports are provided, perhaps on a weekly basis. Thus, students requiring these supports, and the staff who provide them, may meet for Tier 3 sessions from 10:00–10:30 a.m. during Week A and from 1:00–1:30 p.m. during Week B. Because the remainder of the schedule remains fixed from week to week, students would not miss critical but less prioritized content for extended periods.

- Elementary and secondary schools could provide Tier 3 supports during the second halves of instructional blocks. Students receiving Tier 3 interventions could then participate in the first phases of gradual release of responsibility lessons, leaving the class to receive Tier 3 supports while other students complete tasks independently or with peers. As with nearly all decisions about MTSS-based practices, these examples require a cost-benefit analysis.

Schools can creatively schedule Tier 3 supports, such as the following.

- Providing supports when students would otherwise be working independently, such as during workshop, center, or time where students work independently in rotations (daily five time), allowing the teacher to be free to work with and support students individually or in small groups
- Alternating what content the student misses from week to week
- Providing these supports when students are not receiving instruction in the essentials of the grade level

Because extended school days and extended school years are unlikely, and because it's ideal to include these supports during the regular school day, we must creatively find time during the normal school day to provide these supports.

Staff Members Best Positioned to Provide Supports

Another precious resource in our schools is the staff members needed to provide intensive interventions. While we are excited about the potential of blended learning options and the uses of technology to instruct students, we will always need educators to support students, and this includes students requiring tiered supports.

As a rule, we want the most qualified staff members working with the students who are most at risk. Reality will dictate that availability will be another variable to consider, and this may mean that a less-than-optimally-qualified, but highly motivated, staff member is providing supports. For this reason in particular, initial and ongoing professional development must be provided to any and all staff members serving as interventionists.

To find times during the day during which staff members may be available, or can be *made* available, to provide supports to small groups of students, we recommend that schools use a reproducible such as "Staff Availability" (page 47).

The idea behind such a detailed analysis is not to suggest that staff members are not already working at maximum capacity; it simply recognizes that we will require all staff to consider working differently, more efficiently, and perhaps even in different capacities. We unfailingly respect educators' areas of strength and the contracts of bargaining units; infringing on rights is never a consideration. However, there may be thirty minutes of a staff member's day that can be repurposed to provide a targeted support. While we have worked with school secretaries with the will and skill to provide reading intervention to students, we recognize that this may not be a common circumstance. However, perhaps a staff member who is *not* primarily designated to provide instructional supports can complete a task in a thirty-minute block of time that will free a staff member who *is* primarily designated to provide instructional supports to provide a daily intervention. Every thirty-minute time block that can be freed up represents intensive, timely supports for students that would otherwise not be provided.

Resources, Strategies, and Programs Necessary to Meet Student Needs

We firmly believe that *what* educators use with students at risk need not represent as great a challenge as questions associated with *when* and *who*. We simply believe in the power of adults to effect change; we believe that *how* we utilize materials will always be more important than the materials themselves.

This is not to suggest that we should ignore the importance of high-quality resources, strategies, or programs. Carving out time to provide supports and identifying a staff member to provide the supports will likely require a great deal of compromise and effort; do not neglect the *what*.

Potentially powerful materials are lying dormant in schools and districts, and when they are not, they can be acquired at reasonable costs. Identify targeted supports that most specifically meet diagnosed student needs. Homework club, for example, is an appropriate support for a student who needs a safe, structured environment in which to complete work—a student who needs to be nudged to refocus from time to time. But homework club is not an effective support for students who require explicit and intensive reading interventions. However, if the students primarily have deficits in phonics, there may be more appropriate resources, strategies, programs, or supports to use.

We recommend that school leaders begin their identification of *what* resources are needed by drawing on the skills and experiences of their staff members. Effective interventions often fall out of favor, or are only used in special education settings, or have only been thought to be appropriate in certain grade levels. In other words, appropriate interventions may already be present in your school.

- Collectively examine current and past practices to inventory what exists at your school. School districts rarely discard materials, and most have warehouses full of the favored programs of years gone by.

- Visit your district offices and chat with district historians to determine if old programs can be resuscitated.

- Examine the evidence of staff success, both in and outside your school, and ask superstars to share the resources, strategies, and programs that they use.

In general, Tier 2 supports will not require additional material resources. Bloom's mastery learning (Akpan, 2020; Bloom, 1968, 1984) and Richard DuFour, Rebecca DuFour, Robert Eaker, Thomas W. Many, and Mike Mattos's (2016) definitions of PLC practices both propose that Tier 2 represents more time and alternative strategies to support students in mastering grade-level and content essentials. Strategies need not cost money, are not best found in a program, and can be identified through an analysis of student performance. Are there staff members, or individuals or organizations in the community, who have had relatively greater levels of success helping students master specific skills?

While Tier 2 supports typically involve supporting students in their efforts to master specific skills, Tier 3 supports are typically necessary because of deficits in broader domains of foundational skills that were likely an essential standard years ago. A fifth-grade student requiring Tier 2 supports may need a little more time due to difficulties identifying key events in a text from which causes and effects can be determined. A fifth-grade student requiring Tier 3 supports may have difficulty with cause and effect due to the inability to decode single-syllable words.

Tier 3 supports typically require more time, more intensity, and more staff; students will benefit from a more scoped and sequenced (meaning highly organized resources that busy staff members can use with relative ease) and systematic set of materials. This often comes in the form of programs, some of which may already be present in your school or district. Use the reproducible "Resources, Strategies, and Programs" (page 48) to identify what your school already possesses and what you may need to acquire.

Glean items relevant to the domains in the chart from the following sources.

- All classrooms and closets in the school
- District office warehouses
- Other schools in the area

In the domain of behavior, purchasable programs are typically not the answer. Yet, there does exist a rich reservoir of research-based strategies from which educators can draw. Staff members are often strangely disappointed that a secret behavioral program or set of strategies does not exist.

However, there are highly effective strategies that, when used consistently and supported by other key elements of positive behavior, will radically improve student behavior, and they are widely available (Weber, 2018). These strategies can be adopted from educators in your school and from sources in existing behavioral support systems. When completing the reproducible "Resources, Strategies, and Programs," list the behavioral strategies that have proven most successful in your school and school district and that appear most frequently in the research and literature, and commit to using them more effectively and consistently.

Summary

This chapter examined the steps necessary for effective implementation of Tier 2 and Tier 3. Driven by the needs identified at each school, supported by the available resources (human, physical, and financial), and contextualized to the community, these two tiers are key to ensuring the smooth progress of the journey. As we suggested in the introduction to the chapter, additional experts available to assist often provide insights to ensuring a successful road trip. Similarly, the expertise of all educators brought to the task at hand ensures a greater likelihood of all students achieving the desired outcomes.

The next chapter guides schools through a self-analysis and identification of first steps to developing a multitiered system of supports. These steps are intended to facilitate a reflective process through which educators celebrate their successes, build on existing processes and practices, and identify initial tasks. Determining the answers to such questions as, *Where are we going?*, *Where are we now?*, and *What are the next steps?* is a critical and foundational step in school-improvement efforts. Launching initiatives without knowing why changes are necessary, and without validating that successful change is feasible, can negatively impact school culture, imperil the success of the effort, and compromise student learning. Providing a sense of hope built on acknowledging the skills and capacity of the adults working in schools offers the best potential to split from traditional practice and achieve breakthroughs in student outcomes.

Prioritize Content

Just as you prioritize standards in content areas, content areas must also be prioritized. Brainstorm and list the most critical content areas and skills, using the second column to rank the highest-priority contents and skills.

Critical Content Areas and Skills	Priority Rank
1.	
2.	
3.	
4.	
5.	
6.	
7.	
8.	
9.	
10.	

Staff Availability

In the leftmost column, list all staff who are available. In the remaining blocks in the top row, write the times of day, beginning at the start of the school day until the end of the school day. Write in half-hour increments (such as 8:00–8:30 a.m., 8:30–9:00 a.m., and so on).

Staff	Times of the School Day							

Resources, Strategies, and Programs

Scour and glean items relevant to the domains from the following sources.

- All classrooms and closets in the school
- District office warehouses
- Other schools in the area

Log your findings in the chart.

Domain	What or Where	Already Own or Need to Acquire
Phonological awareness		
Phonics		
Advanced phonics		
Fluency		
Vocabulary		
Comprehension		
Early numeracy		
Computation		
Behavior		
Other:		
Other:		

The Road to Success With MTSS © 2023 Solution Tree Press • SolutionTree.com

Visit **go.SolutionTree.com/schoolimprovement** to download this free reproducible.

CHAPTER 3

Where Are We and What Are the Next Steps?

The next step in the journey begins with self-analysis. You can't figure out the route before you know where you are standing right now. This chapter helps you find an answer to the question, *Where are we now?* This step requires courage and candor as schools examine the data and evidence that reflect current realities and states of readiness.

Staff must ask themselves and each other the following questions as they begin moving toward implementation.

- In what areas do our students need the most support?
- In what areas would our staff members benefit from more support?
- Which initiatives would most significantly benefit students and most impact multiple content areas and domains?
- For what initiatives with the MTSS system are we most prepared, in terms of both culture and structures?
- What are the current strengths and needs of staff and students?
- To what extent are all students responding to instruction?
- Are all staff members prepared to accept the change and temporary discomforts associated with MTSS-based practices?

After that self-analysis, evidence and artifacts gathered during the self-analysis will determine the first and next steps for schools and school systems as their leaders begin to systematize their efforts to meet all students' academic and behavioral needs. Determining in which direction to take the first steps of the journey is a critical decision for schools following the MTSS road map. Building in early wins ensures ongoing commitment to being part of the journey and energizes educators to tackle some of the bumps on the road. As authors Teresa Amabile and Steven Kramer (2011) state:

> These small wins matter more because they are so much more likely to occur compared to the big breakthroughs in the world. If we only waited for the big wins, we would be waiting a long time. And we would probably quit long before we see anything tangible come to fruition. What you need instead of the big wins is simply the forward momentum that small wins bring. (p. 21)

This chapter helps you get a clear picture of your current MTSS practices and guides you in determining next steps.

Doing a School Self-Analysis

The notion that focusing on the areas of greatest need yields results is linked to the Pareto principle (DeFeo, 2017), which suggests that identifying and addressing the key elements impeding progress will result in the greatest impact. Ultimately, this process allows for the most efficient use of time and resources. The Pareto principle is derived from the notion that there are generally a few underlying causes that explain the majority of an organization's difficulties (DeFeo, 2017). It's often referred to as the *80:20 rule*, suggesting that 80 percent of our challenges can be addressed by focusing on 20 percent of the causes.

The information gathered in the "MTSS Road Map Self-Analysis" (page 60) tool helps schools identify their areas of greatest need; use it to guide your school as educators determine their current realities and states of readiness. The tool is neither a checklist to ensure full coverage nor a gotcha to point out flaws. Instead, it includes statements of practice that we have helped create, or have observed, in schools throughout North America in which high levels of commitment to and success at improving student learning have been achieved, including staff practices or systems that schools create, employ, and sustain to support student needs. The reproducible "MTSS Road Map Self-Analysis" is simply a way to know where you are so that you can know where you need to go.

These next steps may involve improving school practices in the following areas.

- Culture and climate
- Reading domains
- Mathematics domains
- Writing domains
- Behavioral domains

- Social justice

- Improvements at Tier 1, 2, or 3, or a combination

Keep a couple of things in mind.

- **Try not to become discouraged when completing this self-analysis:**
  This includes when implementing structures related to MTSS or doing
  any work associated with improving the educational opportunities
  for all students. We've been there! We've led continuous improvement
  efforts and continue to do so. Do not beat yourselves up about how far
  you have to go, and don't expect everything to happen immediately or
  all at once.

- **Resist the urge to tackle multiple new initiatives:** Choose wisely,
  do it well, and you can expect your well-chosen and well-implemented
  effort to have a dramatic impact on student learning.

Please note that the self-analysis addresses more than what the professionals in
schools *do*. Educators are also prompted to analyze what they *believe*. Successful
MTSS programs and high-performing schools are based on more than structures—
they are based on cultures of high expectations and high levels of commitment.

Approaches for Completing the Self-Analysis

We recommend that schools invite an external, discreet critical friend to act as
a collaborative partner in this self-analysis. Members of the school staff should
participate in the analysis, both because all staff members have knowledge of a
school's current reality and because all staff members must be committed to and
involved in the collaborative work to fully complete the self-analysis.

Schools may select from several options when completing the self-analysis.

- Individual staff members independently complete the self-analysis and
  then submit their responses to be collated and prepared for analysis.

- Individual staff members independently complete the self-analysis and
  then collaborate with a team to discuss results before submitting team
  responses to be collated and prepared for analysis.

- Teams collaboratively complete the self-analysis and then submit their
  responses to be collated and prepared for analysis.

- The entire school meets to complete the self-analysis, and then collates
  and analyzes responses.

Options When Analyzing the Self-Analysis

As teams begin the next step in the process, they will have an eye toward coalescing around the self-analysis items that were rated. There are also several options for analyzing the data, evidence, and artifacts from the self-analysis.

- **Internal expert team:** This guiding coalition analyzes data, evidence, and artifacts regarding MTSS-related practices and prepares a synthesized report for the broader staff. This team is made up of representatives from key stakeholder groups, such as the following.
    - → Administrative team
    - → Department teams
    - → Grade-level teams
    - → Classified personnel
    - → Clinicians (school nurses, social workers, and so on)
    - → Parents
    - → Students

- **Internal expert groups:** Mixed groups composed of stakeholders from various sections of the school, such as those listed in the *internal expert team* description, analyze data, evidence, and artifacts regarding MTSS-related practices in specified MTSS domains like the following. They then prepare portions of a synthesized report for the guiding coalition and the entire staff.
    - → Culture
    - → Assessment
    - → Data
    - → Core instruction
    - → Interventions
    - → Reading
    - → Mathematics
    - → Writing
    - → English language acquisition
    - → Behaviors
    - → Team meetings and communication
    - → Instructional schedules

- **Externally supported analysis:** Experienced MTSS experts collaborate with staff, guiding the analysis of data, evidence, and artifacts regarding MTSS-related practices. The external team takes final responsibility for preparing a synthesized report for the guiding coalition and the school staff.

We share multiple options for engaging in this process to illustrate that, while determining where we are is essential, it is crucial to take into consideration school size and other logistical and demographic variables when determining how to best achieve that goal.

Dependable Data

Having dependable data sources is critical. It's not good enough to evaluate reading proficiency by counting the number of books taken from the library; an assessment of comprehension would yield better information. It is equally important that the analysis includes identifying staff needs. For staff to become more strategic in their instructional decisions, the identification of gaps in their capacity to differentiate to meet the needs of all learners might need to be addressed. And, it's not too early to plan for how the success of initiatives and next steps will be measured and monitored.

The Three Gaps

Education experts Anne E. Conzemius and Terry Morganti-Fisher (2012) suggest that identifying the areas of greatest need and the resultant priorities for addressing them is best achieved by analyzing three gaps.

1. **The accountability gap** is the difference between today's performance and the performance to which we will be held accountable at some point in the future.

2. **The proficiency gap** is the difference between where you are today and 100 percent of students learning at a rate that enables them to graduate ready for college or a skilled career.

3. **The change-over-time gap** is positive, in that it reveals the difference between the necessary performance data and where you are today in terms of student proficiency.

Analyzing these three gaps assists school leaders and educators when identifying their areas of greatest need and when determining which practices will produce the highest gains. For example, at an elementary school that shows a large percentage of students not reading at or near grade level, an intensive focus on core and supplemental reading supports might have the greatest impact; for a secondary school that shows an increase in office referrals (class removals), an intensive focus on core and supplemental behavioral supports and inclusive practices in core academic courses might lead to the most dramatic and immediate increases in student achievement. Here again, the Pareto principle rings true (DeFeo, 2017).

The Accountability Gap

This is the gap schools and districts most often pursue and satisfies a compliance need. The accountability gap is the difference between current performance and the performance for which the school or students will be held accountable in the future. How this future accountability is determined has the potential to create some angst for staff and derail the progress being made.

This accountability can be neither an arbitrary number arrived at as part of an assumed ongoing growth model (we just add one percent to last year's results, ignoring the students in class today and their relative scores), nor so lax that it does not require much work to achieve. It's best arrived at in a fulsome, data-driven dialogue that looks at numerous factors impacting achievement results.

Teams examine the evidence gathered, discuss those factors that may have impacted the data—for example, the COVID-19 pandemic resulting in lost instructional time and a shift in delivery of instruction—and look for gaps between where they might expect their students to be and where the evidence indicates they are. This conversation is not about identifying adults who didn't succeed in their teaching but instead identifies where the gaps are in the results and what educators might do to remediate those gaps. One way that schools have addressed additional Tier 2 support is through the establishment of *whatever I need* (WIN) time, which is a dedicated block of time (thirty minutes, ideally every day) where students receive timely and targeted instruction designed to impact the gaps identified.

The Proficiency Gap

The proficiency gap addresses the oft-stated goal of all students achieving proficiency, and is commonly referred to as the *commitment gap*. The proficiency gap is the difference between current learning and 100 percent of students learning at a rate that enables them to graduate college and career ready. We often hear that it is unrealistic to ever expect 100 percent of our students to master key content. While only a few sites can claim this success, we maintain that this must be the objective. Put another way: Are you willing to identify those students to whom we should not offer our best—to cut our losses by adding nothing to their skill set so that they are unprepared for their transition to life beyond school? Moreover, you are not setting a goal that all students be on track to attend an Ivy League school. You are setting a goal of academically preparing all students to a level where they could go to college if they want, and they'll be well prepared for whatever path they choose.

Educators planning to use MTSS for addressing academic and behavioral needs as a means of closing gaps are crucial to the success of schools and districts. Among the variety of reasons for considering the importance of MTSS in addressing these gaps, the following sections present three illustrative examples: third-grade reading level, COVID-19's achievement gap, and self-control.

Third-Grade Reading Level Is Key

While districts often spend considerable time and resources addressing how to increase graduation levels (with much of the focus occurring in the high school grades), the research indicates that much of the foundational work (and the key components of MTSS) must occur in the early grades of a student's school life. Professor of sociology Donald J. Hernandez (2011) shares the results of a longitudinal study of nearly four thousand students, which finds that those who do not read proficiently by third grade are four times more likely to leave school without a diploma than proficient readers. For the most challenged readers, those who could not master even the basic skills by third grade, the rate is nearly six times greater. While these struggling readers account for about one-third of the students, they represent more than three-fifths of those who eventually drop out or fail to graduate on time.

COVID-19 and the Achievement Gap

As the impact of the COVID-19 global pandemic continues to be felt in schools, much discussion is occurring around the specifics (and the inequities) of that impact. Richard Rothstein, a distinguished fellow at the Economic Policy Institute, suggests that "the covid-19 pandemic will take existing academic achievement differences between middle-class and low-income students and explode them" (as cited in Strauss, 2020). This will, inevitably, put pressure on various components of a school's MTSS outcomes and may result in, for example, an increase in short-term Tier 2 intervention time as educators work intently and intentionally to decrease the gaps that may have been exacerbated by time away from typical classroom instruction.

Self-Control as a Key Skill

One aspect of MTSS that is essential in ensuring all students achieve the desired outcomes concerns the development of self-regulating behaviors. This developable skill is essential for the student growth. Researchers Jian-Bin Li, Shan-Shan Bi, Yayouk E. Willems, and Catrin Finkenauer (2021) state, "Self-control aids children and adolescents to navigate the challenges during the developmental process to achieve optimal outcomes" (p. 101). As schools work to fully integrate the key aspects of MTSS, it is critical that time be devoted to these other essential skills that often are not as easily measured as academic attributes.

The Change-Over-Time Gap

The change-over-time gap is a positive indicator and is the difference between the necessary performance data and where you are today in terms of student proficiency. This suggests that a student's current proficiency levels are measured against an initial baseline assessment to see if instruction has had a positive or negative impact over time. For example, schools may decide to assess each student's current reading level and compare that to their expected reading level based on their grade. Following an examination of that evidence, an intervention plan could be established for those students who are not at level, with periodic checks to see how they are progressing. This also provides some insight as to whether an intervention is having an impact and is worth continuing.

Taking Action on Next Steps

Moving from goals (identification of need) to next steps requires action. Based on analyses, what information has emerged? What are your top three next steps? Your areas of greatest need? Consolidating the work of these first two sections of the MTSS road map may seem overwhelming, and schools often get stuck here. The temptation to do it all at once is strong, particularly when faced with external pressures that demand change in a short period of time. Remember the Pareto principle and the notion that focusing intensely on a small number of items (20 percent) will address a large portion (80 percent) of the challenges (DeFeo, 2017). How then do you figure out which goals are most important?

Zone analysis helps schools move from need identification to action (Conzemius & Morganti-Fisher, 2012). The strategy involves disaggregating data sources to isolate where improvement is needed and matching the strategies that will best address these gaps: "Without this kind of analysis, all student performance remains lumped into an average, which tells us little about individual student performance and provides almost no guidance on what to do about it" (Conzemius & Morganti-Fisher, 2012, p. 52). A school might use the data sources in table 3.1 to identify areas of greatest need.

TABLE 3.1: DATA SOURCES AND POSSIBLE REVELATIONS

Data Source	Possible Revelation
Academic results from classrooms	Students identified as proficient, beyond proficient, or not yet proficient
	Strategies that worked or didn't work as far as content delivery
	Assessment items that may be ineffective or misaligned
Academic results from external assessments (such as district assessments or benchmarks)	Students identified as proficient, beyond proficient, or not yet proficient
	Whole program evidence as to effective identification of priority learning
Behavior referral data from the office (distinguishing between minor and major offenses)	Effectiveness of behavior instruction and expectations
	Areas of need based on what caused the infractions
	Time of day and day of week
Diagnostics, such as Scales of Independent Behavior–Revised (Bruininks, Woodcock, Weatherman, & Hill, 1996)	Accuracy of information and effectiveness of intervention
Screeners, such as the Philadelphia Urban ACE Survey (Public Health Management Corporation, 2013), SRSS-IE (Ci3T, 2020; Drummond, 1994), and SIBSS (Cook et al., 2011)	Effectiveness of interventions
	Support structures
Teacher and MTSS team feedback	Effectiveness of implemented modifications
	Planning of next steps
Student surveys	Outcomes achieved
	Gathered follow-up evidence

Figure 3.1 (page 58) is an example of how teachers might group their evidence. In this example, the students are sorted based on their achievement of ten learning targets. The team decided that students who met zero to six targets measured as *struggling*, those who met seven to eight targets measured as *progressing*, and those who met nine to ten targets were proficient. The team went further to identify students for whom attendance was a concern (in bold) as that may lead to a separate discussion on strategies to address that gap (in addition to strategies to address the academic deficits).

Struggling		Progressing		Proficient
Aiden	Silas	Adam	Maia	Daphne
Billy	Sophie	Alana	Madison	Madelaine
Dakota		Christian	Natalie	Max
Iris		Cyrus	November	Nia
Jayne		Damian	Shane	
Johnny		Dillon	Spencer	
Julianna		Ellie	Tyra	
Kylie		Jaron	Ulysses	
Maddy		Leah		
Bold = Nonattendees				

Figure 3.1: Example of grouped evidence.

From these data, the team may generate some questions such as the following.

- Why are the struggling students struggling? Why can't we see much growth yet?

- What are we doing well for the students who are progressing? How can we ensure they stay on track?

- For the students who are proficient, how do we extend the learning targets?

As you examine the model schools outlined in the appendix (page 115), do you see practices that would address the challenges you are facing? This may help identify your first or next steps when analyzing your realities to locate goals and discussing methods for addressing them over time. Continuing to devote staff meeting time, collaboration time, and professional development time to addressing challenges and making midcourse corrections will help you achieve your desired outcomes. As you collaborate on the model schools, also celebrate your successes, and look to leverage those as you continue the work. The reproducible "Determining Areas of Greatest Need" (page 65) helps teams summarize what needs to happen during this part of your journey.

Summary

The first step in the journey toward high levels of learning for all students is to determine one's current location. These courageous conversations are a part of the larger—and critically important—topic of school culture. Culture will ultimately be the reason why a school succeeds in guaranteeing that all students graduate from high school ready for college or a skilled career, or alternatively, why school leaders struggle to get improvement efforts started or fail to sustain systematic improvement efforts.

The next chapter describes the steps that schools can take to ensure that good ideas and best intentions translate into high levels of student achievement, as well as help them anticipate what kind of blowback they will get from resisters.

MTSS Road Map Self-Analysis

Rate your school from 1 to 4 on the criteria listed in the following table. Add any and all artifacts, documents, evidence, and data that support your analysis. When there are sub-items embedded in a row, please assign a 1–4 rating to each item and include notes for each item in the space provided.

1. Consistent and effective

2. Fairly consistent and generally effective

3. Inconsistent and occasionally effective

4. Not present or observable

	Rate 1-4	Notes
Every staff member believes that all students can learn at very high levels.		
Students would be likely to share thoughts like the four learning mindsets and skills (Farrington et al., 2012). 1. "I belong in this academic community." 2. "My ability and competence grow with my effort." 3. "I can succeed at this." 4. "This work has value for me."		
All teachers and teams promote, nurture, and reinforce the four learning mindsets and skills (Farrington et al., 2012).		
Teachers are aware of their biases and take actions that represent their belief that all students will meet college and career readiness expectations.		

	Rate 1-4	Notes
Staff members are willing to do whatever it takes to ensure that all students learn at the very highest levels, including but not limited to altering schedules, making courses and curriculum more accessible, reconsidering assignments, scaffolding and differentiating instruction, and adjusting grading and assessment practices.		
Courses and curriculum are accessible to all students, including those from underrepresented and historically minoritized and marginalized groups.		
Instructional strategies are identified and shared that engage all learners and best help students master essential learning targets.		
Our school clearly identifies and articulates, consistently models, and positively reinforces the behaviors that it expects all students to exhibit, including but not limited to the following areas (Farrington et al., 2012). • Mindsets • Social skills • Perseverance • Learning strategies • Academic behaviors		
Every staff member at the school consistently models, corrects, and positively reinforces the behaviors and habits that they expect all students to exhibit.		

page 2 of 5

	Rate 1-4	Notes
School MTSS and collaborative teams consistently use evidence to determine the following. • Which students need additional time and support • Areas in which these identified students most need the additional time and support • Areas in which all students will benefit from additional time and support		
All teachers and teams use assessment, grading, and feedback practices that increase hope, efficacy, achievement, and accuracy, through standards-based grading. • Clear learning targets and success criteria • Assessments aligned to learning targets • Formative assessments provide feedback to students and teachers prior to the summative • Feedback aligned to learning targets and reported in proficiency levels (not percentages) • Opportunities to demonstrate growth in understanding • Grades authentically reflect what they know (not how they got there)		
An increasing percentage of all class assessments are done as follows. • Administered commonly by all team members • Used formatively with students • Used to collectively inform teaching and learning		

	Rate 1-4	Notes
An increasing percentage of all class assessments include the following. • Pretests that assess the prerequisite skills that students should possess to successfully learn upcoming content or the students' knowledge of upcoming content • Mid-unit tests that assess student progress part of the way through a unit, but well before the end of the unit, so that timely interventions can be provided • End-of-unit tests that allow teams to know which students will continue to require support in mastering certain essential learning outcomes even though a new unit of instruction is set to begin • Reassessments to measure progress students have made after reteaching and relearning have occurred • Formal or informal checks for understanding including exit tickets and mid-lesson comprehension checks • Progress monitoring that more frequently and validly monitors students' response to intervention, and, when errors are analyzed, can also diagnose students' needs		
The school has built times into the instructional day for students to receive supplemental Tier 2 supports *in addition to* core Tier 1 instruction *and* differentiated instruction provided by grade-level and content-alike teams.		

	Rate 1-4	Notes
The school provides timely, targeted, and intensive Tier 3 supports to students with significant needs in foundational skills as soon as possible upon discovering these needs.		
The school has inventoried all staff members' availabilities and abilities and assigned them to directly provide supports to students, with initial and ongoing professional development provided.		
Teams meet twice monthly to coordinate their efforts on behalf of students.		
Team processes ensure that information is efficiently documented and communicated to all stakeholders.		

Source: Farrington, C. A., Roderick, M., Allensworth, E., Nagaoka, J., Keyes, T. S., Johnson, D. W., et al. (2012). Teaching adolescents to become learners: The role of noncognitive factors in shaping school performance—A critical literature review. *Chicago: University of Chicago Consortium on Chicago School Research.*

page 5 of 5

Determining Areas of Greatest Need

Use this guide to determine relative priorities in establishing your areas of greatest need. Remember the Pareto principle—focusing intensely on a small number of items (20 percent) will address a large portion (80 percent) of the challenges—to ensure proper focus and maximum impact (DeFeo, 2017).

Relative Goal Priority

Relative goal priority rating is as follows.

1. Not required at this time (or may be impacted by focus on other items)
2. Could be part of a future plan if data indicate
3. Will have an impact but should not be a first step
4. Absolutely needed to improve student outcomes

From the MTSS Road Map Self-Analysis, Our Team Generated the Following List	Relative Goal Priority	Each Item Listed as Academic or Behavioral
1.		
2.		
3.		
4.		

5.		
6.		
7.		
8.		
9.		
10.		
11.		

Zone Analysis

The following data sources will help us identify our top three areas of greatest need.

- Academic results from classrooms
- Academic results from external assessments
- Behavior referral data from the office

The case study information in the appendix (page 115) highlights these areas for us to consider or explore further.

Area 1:

Area 2:

Area 3:

As a result of the analysis of the model school information, our goals for the next school year are as follows. (Limit your goals and immediate next steps to no more than three. Your school may not have three total.)

1.

2.

3.

Source: Adapted from Conzemius, A. E., & Morganti-Fisher, T. (2012). More than a SMART goal: Staying focused on student learning. *Bloomington, IN: Solution Tree Press.*
DeFeo, J. A. (2017). Juran's quality handbook: The complete guide to performance excellence *(7th ed.). New York: McGraw-Hill.*

CHAPTER 4

What Stops Do We Make
Along the Way?

Once schools have examined successful school models, analyzed their current levels of performance as it relates to MTSS, and identified areas of greatest need and highest-leverage solutions, they must initiate, monitor, revise, and sustain their MTSS-based school improvement practices. This is where the ten steps come in.

Knowing the implementation process and where you are in it is crucial. If a school does not determine how teachers will know *if* or *when* they have successfully reached a goal—or specific areas in which success has been achieved and others in which midcourse corrections are necessary—there are several potential unfortunate outcomes.

- Pushback from less-than-enthusiastic stakeholders may undermine efforts, or some may advocate terminating improvement efforts.

- Less-than-optimally successful areas will not receive the supports required to get them back on track, leading to stalled progress, frustration, and the risk of a failed initiative.

- Particularly successful areas will not be identified, celebrated, and replicated.

- The appropriate time to initiate next steps will not be recognized, leading to missed opportunities to meet more of students' needs.

There will be stops along the way as you move toward your ultimate destination of a comprehensive system of supports in which all students get what they need and are on track to graduate college and career ready. The ten steps detailed in this chapter will empower educators to check the status of their progress at the stops along the way.

Students will be more motivated to learn when they observe the growth achieved through their hard work. Educators will respond in the same way. We have found that even initially reluctant staff will develop a firmer commitment to new ideas when they witness or experience success. That success, known as a mastery experience, increases an individual's self-efficacy (Bandura, 1994; Bryant, 2017). To maximize the chances of this occurring, schools must have systems that establish goals, measure progress toward those goals, and communicate progress, celebrating or making course corrections as appropriate. Following the ten steps to success will ensure these actions occur.

Following the Ten Steps to Success

Building and sustaining a multitiered system of supports involves multiple processes, including the following.

- Guiding staff through the change process, including discussions about why the change is necessary, what the change will involve, how the change will be supported, and how the success of the change will be measured

- Reflecting on and refining core Tier 1 instruction for both academics and behavior

- Identifying students in need, and diagnosing the causes of their difficulties

- Researching, acquiring, and gaining competency with intervention strategies and resources

- Researching, acquiring, and gaining competency with tools for monitoring student progress

- Developing systems for a cyclical problem-solving process

Determining which of those elements have not yet been addressed, which have been initiated, which have been established, and which have been successful are critical elements of an MTSS road map, for which the steps to success will provide guidance.

The ten steps to success are given here and in the reproducible "Steps to Success for MTSS-Based Practice" (page 94). The steps help ensure that the implementation process successfully leads to improved staff performance and student outcomes.

1. Clearly define the desired outcomes and establish completion dates.

2. Identify key interim and final benchmarks.

3. Research and identify the information, resources, and professional learning necessary to meet the interim and final benchmarks.

4. Acquire and distribute the required information and resources and provide the professional learning.

5. Anticipate and prepare for roadblocks and obstacles.

6. Initiate the MTSS-based practices.

7. Gather and analyze evidence.

8. Make midcourse corrections.

9. Provide targeted and positive supports to teams and individuals.

10. Persevere, measure, and celebrate success.

We draw on the work of systems scientist Peter Senge (1990) and education author Michael Fullan (2010) in crafting a systems approach to this work given that Senge is a very respected and frequently referenced leader in systems thinking across all fields and Fullan is the recognized expert in systems thinking in education.

In each of the ten steps detailed in the following sections, we run through an ongoing example—a middle school, in which a significant number of students are not reading at grade level. Although this example is focused on a middle school, these needs and the corresponding steps for success can apply to elementary, middle, and high schools.

Step 1: Clearly Define the Desired Outcomes and Establish Completion Dates

The first step is to clearly define the desired outcomes and establish completion dates. This is one of the three critical MTSS elements: problem solving to determine the appropriate course of action. Our firm belief that behavior and academics are inextricably linked leads to the establishment of goals that impact both of these areas in our work with schools. Identifying your top three challenges and then engaging all educators at your site in planning will ensure that the necessary focus and required resources are brought to the work.

We recommend that educators set ambitious goals, known to some as *big hairy audacious goals* (BHAGs; Collins, 2001). Each goal must be accompanied by reasonable completion dates. We recommend limiting goals to three or fewer so that educators can focus their limited time on a finite number of initiatives, thereby avoiding fatigue and becoming stretched too thin. These desired outcomes should not simply define what changes will be made or processes introduced by staff; they must also define the measurable outcomes that will be achieved. For our middle school example, English teachers, in partnership with special education staff, have determined that deficits in fluency and comprehension are the root cause of the inability of large numbers of students to read at grade level. In this case, the desired outcome (the BHAG) is for all students to read at grade level, with progress assessed at the conclusion of each grading period for individual students and all students who are at risk.

Being intentional about our goals will provide the clarity needed. You might start with a goal that says, "We will implement direct instruction (instruction that emphasizes a step-by-step approach while focusing on the essential learning) in mathematics." Using the three gaps mentioned from the previous section (page 53) may help schools determine their priority goals and establish a timeline for reaching them. The goal identified here could have both short-term (end-of-unit, for example) and long-term (end-of-year reporting, for example) checks for progress. This may ensure a better process for delivering mathematics content but may not impact student learning. Adding "so that all students are able to master the most highly prioritized standards at grade level as measured by common assessments" leads to the necessary focus. In this goal, you can also layer in strategies for any subgroups of students for whom the gaps may be larger, ensuring that those gaps are closed.

As is the case when creating common assessments from which teachers will backward plan to drive instructional practices, educators must begin with the end goal of MTSS-based improvement efforts in mind in order to define and drive professional practice. Leaders must also courageously and confidently communicate these goals to staff. We recommend that communication takes many forms: one-to-one with individual staff members, during small-group collaborative team meetings, at whole-staff meetings, and through written communications (such as email). These communications reinforce the why, how, and what of improvement efforts. There is no such thing as too much communication.

Step 2: Identify Key Interim and Final Benchmarks

The next step is to identify key interim and final benchmarks. Interim benchmarks are established so that midcourse corrections can be made. Final benchmarks are established so that you can determine when you have met your goals. The goal in step 1 is more global; in step 2, educators must specify the outcomes that will serve as evidence of achieving the BHAGs. For example, in the scenario introduced in step 1, the global BHAG is that students will read on grade level. In step 2, fluency and comprehension would be monitored much more frequently, approximately every two weeks, using oral reading fluency tests for fluency and accuracy rates and tests of comprehension assessed through informal reading inventories. Interim benchmarks could be administered at the conclusion of each month, and final benchmarks would be at the end of the school year. Success would be judged by students making adequate progress (as measured by student trends of progress exceeding the norm-based aim line) and by students meeting end-of-grade-level expectations for fluency rate and comprehension.

Since the efficacy of interventions is determined through targeted progress monitoring of individual students' responses to those interventions, educators should also consider other methods of benchmarking success. They should ask a question such as, "What improvements would occur as a result of our successful implementation of this MTSS-based practice?" Examples of quantifiable outcomes follow.

- Improved performance on common assessments
- Improved completion rates on classwork and homework
- Improved attendance rates
- Improved attendance
- Improvements in student responses on student surveys

Educators can also quantify more qualitative evidence that students report and that staff and parents monitor, including the following.

- Demonstration of prosocial behaviors such as cooperation and self-control
- Rates of participation or other forms of engagement
- Frequency of positive adult-to-student and student-to-student interactions
- Observations of improved organization
- Observations of more positive mindsets

Gather these data for all students. You can acquire free, valid, and reliable monitoring tools for mathematics and reading from Acadience Learning (www.acadience learning.org). There are other for-fee monitoring tools referenced in the appendix (page 115). For tools for monitoring behavior, please see *Behavior: The Forgotten Curriculum* (Weber, 2018).

Step 3: Research and Identify the Information, Resources, and Professional Learning Necessary

Educators should next research and identify the information, resources, and training necessary to meet those interim and final benchmarks. For our middle school example, a site would benefit from professional learning on the characteristics of fluency and comprehension and on how to identify students with fluency and comprehension needs, including simple assessment tools that would confirm such a need exists and that monitor student progress in these areas. Affordable and even free resources exist for this purpose. Additionally, the staff would need instructional materials that would provide support to students in the areas of fluency and comprehension. There are, again, affordable and free resources available; although, with a modest expenditure, staff would have a program to use that provides more guidance in using the lessons with students. Staff will need initial and ongoing professional learning supports so that the investment of time and money in these resources, on behalf of learners with significant vulnerabilities in reading, is maximally impactful.

Staff members should find research and literature about the highest-leverage solutions for their areas of greatest need, as well as examples of schools and settings in which these solutions have thrived. The principal should take the lead in this area in collaboration with members of the MTSS team and staff at the district office who have relative expertise and experience with reading.

As noted, the MTSS team should research programs and talk with schools that have experienced success meeting students' reading needs to find materials that staff will use with students. Again, there are free resources available, although these require that staff commit more time in the preparation of lessons; moderately priced options exist that are already scoped and sequenced and with guidance (like proposed teacher scripts) provided for educators. While educators are certainly capable of designing and delivering these types of instruction, the same staff who provide these types of supports often have other duties and responsibilities, so the additional guidance is beneficial. Given that there are many resources or programs that can lead to success with the proper implementation and monitoring, we hesitate to provide specific recommendations, although case studies at the conclusion of the book do offer real-world examples.

Lastly, school leaders must identify which professional learning from outside experts is required and worthwhile and which professional learning staff members can conduct on their own. School leaders should refer to their MTSS self-analysis, which inventories staff members' skills and experiences, as well as collaborate with the district office to determine if professional learning supports can be provided internally or if an outside expert is necessary. At times, the MTSS team may determine that a colleague from their system is preferable, whereas at other times, an outside voice may be necessary even if the expertise exists in-house, assuming there is a budget for this professional learning. The team should use their judgment and discretion when making this decision.

While we strongly believe that most schools and districts are filled with educators who possess the expertise, skills, and experiences from which others can benefit, we also find that outside experts and guidance can most definitely inspire and inform change. Cynicism regarding professional learning usually reflects the quality, ongoing support, and actual implementation associated with the professional learning someone has experienced in the past; it does not negate the absolute need for professional development to continually enhance educators' capacities.

Step 4: Acquire and Distribute the Required Information and Resources and Provide the Professional Learning

The identification of needed information, resources, and professional learning is not enough. School leaders must next interact with members of the support staff at the school and district office who will perform the critical tasks of finding the best price, processing paperwork in a timely manner, and scheduling the delivery of materials. The principal will take the lead on the following tasks.

- Reaching out to fiscal services and curriculum staff at the district office to identify funding and budgets for resources

- Supporting office staff in completing the appropriate paperwork, ensuring that paperwork gets to the right people in a timely manner

- Working with professional learning and human resources staff to identify staff, secure funding for their time, and schedule substitutes with funding for the number of staff and days necessary (or funding for after-school training if this proves to be the better option)

The acquisition and distribution of the required information and materials is too often an undervalued step. We have worked in and with schools whose efforts have been stalled because of the following reasons.

- The program was prohibitively expensive (often because the incorrect products were recommended for purchase or more products or materials than necessary were recommended for purchase).

- Program materials have not arrived by the predetermined and planned launch date.

- Professional learning cannot be scheduled (trainers are not available or substitute teachers cannot be secured).

To avoid these problems, we recommend that school leaders devote ample time to meeting face-to-face with support staff members from purchasing, finance, and distribution divisions so that they are part of the team, and so that they understand the school's mission and adopt the same sense of urgency about the necessity of all students learning at high levels that is expected of the educators in the school.

In the middle school example, the principal would ensure that the correct type and quantity of resources (both curricular and assessment) for each domain of reading was purchased out of the correct budgets, district office staff processed and expedited the purchase orders, and professional learning was ready to be provided as soon as resources arrived on campus.

Step 5: Anticipate and Prepare for Roadblocks

Roadblocks will certainly arise, so it's important to be prepared for them. Try to predict, from anecdotes of others' experiences, what these challenges may be and collectively acknowledge that roadblocks and obstacles are inevitable (Buffum et al., 2012). Successfully persevering through predictable challenges separates success from frustration (Shinde, 2020).

There are several roadblocks that may emerge.

- **Staff may not feel prepared to be successful:** To address this potential roadblock, ensure that both initial and ongoing professional learning is provided. Schedule visits by administrators and support staff (coaches) to see the MTSS-based practice in action, and check in with staff. Bring together staff who frequently implement the initiatives to share and collaborate.

- **Management and utilization of data may be cumbersome or overwhelming:** Work with district office staff to check on the availability of software that can support data management and analysis. Set aside staff time for the review of data. Assign the preparation of data reports to the MTSS team to make staff's interpretations of data more seamless.

- **There may not be sufficient data to inform the success or lack of success of an initiative:** Proactively identify the data to examine and determine what tools to use to gather data. Set and faithfully follow a schedule to administer these brief assessments to applicable students.

- **The data may indicate that success is not yet occurring:** Initially, establish and reinforce a culture and expectation that the initiative will result in success, while being mindful there will likely need to be shifts along the way. Be courageous in making shifts. Promote positive mindsets.

- **Students and parents may not be terribly excited about participating in supplemental supports:** Dedicate initial and ongoing time to meet with students and parents to explain the rationale for supplemental supports and the ramifications a lack of support has for the student. Regularly communicate and celebrate progress (in the specific area of need and in other areas, such as behavior and grades in core classes) and promote positive mindsets. Genuinely express your beliefs in the ultimate success of students.

There are several other ways to prepare for roadblocks.

- **Frequently check in with one another:** Principals and other school leaders must get out of the office, ask questions, make observations, gauge the school's climate, and examine early evidence to be in a position to proactively address a challenge.

- **Set aside fiscal resources:** Use them to support the additional materials or professional learning that may be required.

- **Set aside time for town-hall-style meetings to discuss challenges and solutions:** Leadership teams and guiding coalitions should make checking in on the success of the change a priority during meetings.

Difficulties will emerge. Maintaining patient persistence while managing stress is a key role in the MTSS-based change practice for school leaders and for the entire staff. The most precious of resources is time. If and when possible, give staff members the gift of time to collaborate, reflect, and recharge.

Let's apply the elements of this step to the middle school example that we've been revisiting throughout the chapter. The MTSS team should ensure that staff know how to improve fluency and comprehension and how to use provided resources. Establish a schedule to regularly monitor progress using simple, oral reading fluency and comprehension assessments, and organize the data in accessible reports. Schedule meetings with the interventionists who provide and analyze data, gather questions, share ideas, and provide staff with needed supports. Share the progress of students receiving fluency and comprehension supports with all staff.

Step 6: Initiate the MTSS-Based Practices

At some point, schools must begin. Even though educators may not feel ready and think that there is more that could be done to prepare, the MTSS-based practice must be initiated. We recommend that school leaders be transparent about the fact that everyone involved will learn while doing. It is time to set a launch date and commit to revisiting and revising the plan as data become available. Launching any initiative, including MTSS-based practices, always benefits from specific habits.

- **Leaders must follow through with teams and with individuals in the school:** Staff members must feel supported, and they must feel as though the initiative, now launched, will be supported. Building individual and collective capacities can enhance this sense of feeling supported. Specifically speaking, professional learning cannot end once the MTSS-based practice begins; educators must continue to learn, through both formal (after-school, half-day, and full-day training) and informal (one-on-one conversations, asynchronous electronic dialogues, books, and articles) means.

- **It is important to celebrate early victories:** Identifying and sharing positive results shows that it's possible to be successful when implementing an initiative. Early victories are motivating for every single stakeholder involved, so it's important for leaders to capitalize on opportunities to celebrate early successes and communicate positive results widely (van de Rijt, Kang, Restivo, & Patil, 2014). As the initiative is getting under way, examine progress-monitoring data early and often and share and celebrate student gains. In our middle school example, use short oral-reading probes (usually sixty seconds) to measure student gains in reading rate and accuracy and share successes with students, parents, and staff. Take time to acknowledge the hard work of staff and students and honor the positive mindsets that are necessary to persevere in the work.

- **On initiating the planned MTSS-based practice, all stakeholders must commit to revisiting what led to launching the practice in the first place:** If schools are committed to all students learning at high levels, and if there are students in the school not reading at grade level because of (in our example) needs in the areas of fluency and comprehension, then something must be done. Leaders must readdress the why, what, and how of the change. Why did everyone agree that the efforts were necessary? What behaviors and actions are necessary to meet goals? How will successes be measured? Staff members are predictably and understandably going to raise these questions. Guiding coalitions must proactively revisit them. The MTSS team serves as the guiding coalition; they bring the energy and expertise to the work, and they communicate with the stakeholders throughout the school community. Ultimately, they monitor, manage, and motivate the initiative to success (DuFour et al., 2016).

A critical task for the MTSS team is creating schedules for staff and students in an impacted school day for interventions to occur and securing physical spaces in which the supports will be provided.

One final note on step 6: when beginning an initiative like providing supplemental support to students in need of fluency and comprehension supports, look at the core. Look at Tier 1. Determine whether there are shifts to make in the way in which first, best instruction is provided in these areas of reading, in current and previous grade levels, so that fewer students may be at risk in fluency and comprehension in the future.

Step 7: Gather and Analyze Evidence

In step 2, the key interim and final benchmarks were identified. For example, a school with a goal of improving students' oral reading fluency may establish a final benchmark of 100 percent of students scoring at the Benchmark and Strategic levels, with no students scoring at the Intensive level. Given that 40 percent of students were scoring at the Intensive level mid-year (based on the regular screening of all students to proactively identify students most in need), and given that there are four months remaining in the year, a goal is set that the percentage of students scoring at the Intensive level will be reduced by ten points each month.

In this step, school teams gather and analyze evidence related to students' oral reading fluency rates and share results with all staff each month. This allows staff to monitor the progress of individual students and the efficacy of instruction and intervention for all students. Analyses of results for individual students as well as groups of students with higher and lower relative rates of growth are conducted. Screening and monitoring are two of the three critical elements of MTSS.

We recommend that school leaders establish interim check-ins at key decision points. For example, while oral reading fluency rates are gathered, reported, and analyzed every month, the school staff may commit to analyzing data at three-month intervals to identify which students and grade levels may require additional supports and make decisions about resource reallocation. Change is embraced and sustained if educators know that the success of the school's efforts is measured and lessons learned are acted on in a timely and direct manner.

We do not provide specifics because so many tools can lead to success, but the case studies in the appendix (page 115) offer real-world examples.

Step 8: Make Midcourse Corrections

The purpose for gathering and analyzing evidence of the success of MTSS-based practices is to enable educators to make midcourse corrections. MTSS teams—the guiding coalition of this critical function of a school—engage in a cyclical problem-solving process. Problem solving is one of the three critical elements of MTSS. At times, school teams conduct analyses without the willingness to make adjustments. Such decisions require courage; when evidence suggests that current efforts are not resulting in adequate levels of improvement, educators must boldly revise the plan. Such decisions also require prudence; we are not suggesting plans be abandoned altogether. The why that originally justified the change remains the same; minor shifts in the what and how may be necessary to increase the rates at which improvements occur. If an improvement effort does not initially result in the type of progress and success you expect, then don't lose heart; make a midcourse correction and persevere. It is more likely that a minor shift, instead of a major shift, will suffice if analyses of success occur at appropriate intervals.

While you do not want to make rash changes, you also do not want to wait. Let's revisit our middle school fluency-and-comprehension example. If no students in a small group of students receiving comprehension supports are making progress after two cycles of progress monitoring, and if the interventionist notes that the students seem to labor with rate and accuracy when students read aloud, then MTSS team representatives and the interventionist may determine that this group of students may benefit more from a fluency support than from a comprehension support. This represents a minor shift; the targeted skill of the intervention has shifted. This contrasts with the major shift of concluding that the students are not responding to interventions and that a formal evaluation to determine eligibility for special education is necessary.

Another minor shift may be in the frequency of progress monitoring. The site or the team may determine that monthly progress monitoring is not providing timely enough evidence to inform decisions for the progress of individual students and the health and efficacy of the intervention program as a whole. Before implementing a major (and perhaps unnecessary) shift to the entire intervention program, a more minor shift of twice-monthly progress monitoring may be preferable.

Teams of educators can help prepare for the success of midcourse corrections by brainstorming possible scenarios in advance.

- What adjustments will we need to make if certain grade levels or content areas require more support?

- What adjustments will we need to make if success is reached sooner than expected?

- What adjustments will we need to make if more students need support than we have time and personnel to provide support?

- What adjustments will we need to make if a majority of students are not responding to instruction or intervention?

The key, as is so often the case, is a willingness and capacity to respond flexibly. It is essential to plan on making shifts in priorities when interim benchmark targets have not been reached. Such transitions may involve reprioritizing supports and resources and should not be delayed.

Evidence-informed midcourse corrections may involve providing targeted and positive supports to teams and individuals and may require crucial conversations.

Step 9: Provide Targeted and Positive Supports to Teams and Individuals

Conflict is inevitable when making significant changes in education. Conflict can be a productive experience, and may even be a requirement of substantive, transformational improvement. When educators ask questions and question decisions, we consider this engagement, not resistance.

When analysis of data associated with MTSS-based practices reveals a need, staff must exercise the courage to open a true dialogue, proactively addressing shortfalls and developing an action plan. Such dialogues need not be punitive or evaluative. Start by assuming the best of intentions in our colleagues. Staff leaders should anticipate defensiveness and consider that a cynic may simply be a frustrated idealist; the more cynical one seems, the more idealistic one likely used to be. Rediscover that idealism and find common ground and mutual purpose. Once consensus on an MTSS-based practice to improve student learning is reached, participation is mandatory.

Targeted and positive supports may involve and necessitate more professional development, more individualized attention, or more material resources—or a more direct conversation may be required. It's possible that a clarification of what is, and what is not, expected of staff must occur. Difficulties and disagreements, in our experience, sometimes occur because participants were unclear about what was expected. For example, a teacher feels that the instructional planners dictate what must be done daily, when in fact they only define what students must know and be able to do by the end of the unit and serve as a repository of resources from which teams may choose to draw. Another example: a consensus on instruction that involves a gradual release of responsibility is misinterpreted to signify expectations for rigid instructional techniques.

Let's revisit the middle school fluency-and-comprehension example. Some staff may lament that students are missing their class to receive support. Remind them reading is fundamental. Staff, students, and parents may be concerned that the students are unable to participate in an elective because they are in a support class that provides fluency and comprehension supports. Remind them that difficulties in reading will impact students in every course in school and for the rest of their lives and that early intervention therefore enables greater participation in electives. Some staff may be concerned that, after several weeks or even months, the student has not yet reached grade-level proficiency and that parent permission to conduct a formal evaluation to determine special education eligibility should be pursued. Show them that the student is making adequate progress in response to the intervention (if this is, in fact, true) and that they are on track to reach grade-level proficiency. MTSS- and RTI-based practices work; our skill and commitment to the process is the most important variable.

When more extensive conversations are required, a safe environment for honest dialogue is critical. Consider these ways of creating safety and building trust.

- Staff leaders ideally meet in their colleagues' space (such as a classroom), not in the principal's office. When meeting in the principal's office is the best option, sit with colleagues; do not face off from behind a desk.

- Share the topic that will be discussed prior to meeting, allowing colleagues to prepare, thereby avoiding surprises.

- Start the dialogue by sharing your thought processes that have led to the conversation, and using facts (data, evidence, and research related to the MTSS-based practice).

- Provide timely, positive follow-up. Educators need to know that their staff leaders will follow through on commitments.

Any time you have a productive conversation, celebrate that success. Celebrating success is crucial.

Step 10: Persevere, Measure, and Celebrate Success

Step 10 involves leading and managing the entire process of change—the entire MTSS-based practice. It also involves transitioning from one critical practice to another, such as from an exclusive focus on reading (as in the middle school example that we have referenced through the ten steps) and behavior in Tier 2 and Tier 3 to expanding tiered supports to other academic areas.

There will always be new challenges in education, a profession in which continuous improvement is a necessary reality for staff and students, so it is essential that successes be validated and celebrated. Reflection should also take place.

- What attributes of the MTSS-based practice contributed to success?

- What revisions should be made in the future to proactively anticipate roadblocks and obstacles?

- What deficits in student learning and staff knowledge may have emerged in the endeavor that can inform our next MTSS-based practice?

MTSS can and will work; it's among the most proven and research-based initiatives in which schools can engage (Hattie, 2012). The leadership, support, and perseverance of the guiding coalition that is the MTSS team will make the difference between success and frustration.

Dealing With Pushback

The remainder of this chapter identifies and describes possible pushback from stakeholders that we can anticipate and provides guidance on how educators can successfully respond. Our ideas in the sections that follow derive predominantly from the invaluable resource "The Psychology of Resistance to Change" (Rehman et al., 2021).

The Tight-Loose Debate

One likely pressure point for staff members in any change process is the tight-loose debate, which must be addressed, defined, and revisited. School leaders must define which expectations associated with school practices are *tight*, or non-negotiable, and which are appropriately *loose*, or negotiable (DuFour et al., 2016). It is impossible and unproductive for educators and for students for everything to be tight. It is equally inappropriate for everything to be loose.

A clear understanding of what is non-negotiable, and why, is absolutely critical. For example, a sound Tier 1 program, whether in the domain of academics or behavior, is required to achieve a guaranteed, viable curriculum. We believe that rigid pacing guides inhibit flexibility and opportunities to differentiate. Flexible pacing guides, driven by prioritized standards that students must learn in a commonly taught unit with student learning measured by common assessments, are necessary. See table 4.1 for ideas of how to respond to pushback about the tight-loose debate. Ultimately, establishing and maintaining an MTSS-based set of supports for students is a must; it's tight. The ways in which teams implement MTSS is most certainly dependent on the contexts, needs, and realities of the site; it's loose.

TABLE 4.1: RESPONDING TO COMMON TIGHT-LOOSE DEBATE PUSHBACK

Possible Pushback	Possible Response
"We can just provide interventions in class. We don't need to pull students to provide Tier 3 interventions."	"Teachers are amazing. But when it comes to providing daily, intensive, targeted interventions to students who have significant deficits in foundational reading skills, we're going to leverage interventionists. This also allows us to serve students from multiple classrooms at the same time in a separate space."
"Why do we need to have the same behavioral expectations, and why do we need centrally documented behavioral incidents? I have a unique style. I don't want to change."	"Please be you and have a unique personality. However, students see multiple staff members every day in multiple spaces, and we cannot help them succeed if there are different rules in different classes and settings. Further, if we don't know students' behavioral needs, we cannot collectively and proactively respond to trends and meet a student's individual needs before they escalate."
"Why do we need to have common standards-based grading and retake policies?"	"Departments, courses, and grade levels will have unique approaches to grading and reassessment that make sense to students' ages and the standards of the content area, but parents and students deserve and will expect common policies."

Behavior Instruction

Another predictable area in which school leaders may experience pushback from internal stakeholders is in the area of teaching students how to behave. Some people do not believe it is their responsibility to teach the behaviors that students must display while at school, or to teach the behaviors that will enable them to learn how to learn (Blad, 2020). Our question would then be: If not us, then who?

If we are not satisfied with student behavior, and we believe that behavior impacts student learning, then what are our options? Rather, we must collectively assume responsibility for improving behavior and collaboratively support students and one another. Improving student behavior is not easy, but it is possible. The social science behind improving behavior has a larger and more robust research base than any academic domain, with the possible exception of reading. It's not a lack of skill that prevents success in this arena but a lack of will (Dweck, Walton, & Cohen, 2014; Farrington et al., 2012). Principals also report in surveys that they favor the teaching of SEL, but time constraints and lack of teacher training are major barriers (Schwartz, 2019).

Student motivation, or more accurately, a lack of student motivation and engagement, is commonly mentioned as a reason for student difficulties, and as a reason for the failure of improvement efforts. However, educators can have an enormous impact on student motivation. And according to the leading educational psychologists in the world, such as Carol S. Dweck and colleagues (2014), students can be taught to be motivated:

> When these non-cognitive factors [mindsets, social skills, perseverance, learning strategies, academic behaviors] are in place, students will look—and be—motivated. In fact, these non-cognitive factors constitute what psychological researchers call *motivation*, and fostering these mindsets and self-regulation strategies is what psychological researchers typically mean by *motivating* students. [Italics in original]

Students are motivated and engaged when they believe that standards are relevant, when they have choice, when they have relationships with teachers, when they have opportunities to collaborate with peers, when teachers model effective social and academic behaviors, and when schools nurture a growth mindset (Dweck et al., 2014; Farrington et al., 2012). We can have a significant impact on student motivation if we accept responsibility for teaching students behavior skills. See table 4.2 for ideas of how to respond to pushback about behavior instruction.

TABLE 4.2: RESPONDING TO COMMON BEHAVIOR INSTRUCTION PUSHBACK

Possible Pushback	Possible Response
"It's not our job to teach behavior. We have too many academic standards to teach as it is."	"If someone else were going to teach behavioral skills, that would have already occurred. We are the answer we've been waiting for. If we want to teach academic skills, the simultaneous teaching of behavior skills must be part of that."
"We don't have time to teach behaviors."	"Research is clear: behavioral skills are as important as academic skills for student success in schools, college, career, and life. If we need to further prioritize the academic skills that all students should master, let's complete that task so there is time and space during class time to teach, nurture, practice, assess, and provide feedback on behavioral skills."
"I guess we should teach behavioral skills, but classroom teachers shouldn't do it. Can't specialists or administrators do it?"	"Classroom teachers are the best adults to teach the behavioral skills that students need to be successful in their class. If students are not studying well for tests or using their time wisely, classroom teachers ought to be the ones to teach these skills for their class."

Assessment Frequency

MTSS-based practices require evidence. Evidence requires assessment, which comes with a plethora of connotations in education, including that there is not enough time for assessments and there is never enough assessment. The assessment paradox, mentioned earlier, claims that we assess too much and yet do not have the data required to inform our work.

Time spent assessing up front can save time later, however.

- **Inventory the assessments you currently administer:** Check that the timely information that is needed to ensure that all students learn at high levels is being gathered but without redundancies and inefficiencies. Use the reproducible "Inventory Tool for Assessments" (page 96) for this purpose.

- **Unit preassessments reveal gaps in student knowledge of required skills:** Those are gaps that will likely necessitate interventions in the unit. This screening reveals which students have significant deficits that will almost certainly cause them to experience difficulties in the year, at some time and in some content area. Initiating supports immediately saves time and preserves students' belief in their own efficacy. Preassessments can also reveal that students already possess knowledge of content in upcoming units. By compacting content, educators can avoid teaching content students already understand, thereby allowing time for more depth of study or more practice with other content.

- **Preteach prerequisites before and at the beginning of units to fill gaps:** When preassessments reveal there are gaps in the prerequisite knowledge that students need to be successful in a unit, dedicate time at the beginning of the unit to preteaching these skills. If it makes more sense, dedicate time *in* the unit for the preteaching of prerequisite skills at a time that immediately precedes the new content for which the prerequisite skills are needed.

Leaders must have conversations about these benefits with staff members who feel that there is not enough time for more assessment. They must help educators with the practical steps required to inventory assessments, link instruction and assessments, and screen and preassess in a successful way. See table 4.3 (page 88) for ideas of how to respond to pushback about how much assessment occurs.

TABLE 4.3: RESPONDING TO COMMON ASSESSMENT FREQUENCY PUSHBACK

Possible Pushback	Possible Response
"We can't possibly assess more. We already have too much to grade."	"Don't grade all parts of tasks or don't grade in the same ways as we have in the past. Instead, use highlight grading, in which you highlight the portion of the assignment that needs student attention, and students are responsible for analyzing their errors. Only grade and provide feedback on specific elements of the task, like only grading for word choice instead of grammar and spelling in student writing."
"Students don't seem to take grades and feedback seriously."	"Involve students. Have students self-assess using a provided rubric and success criteria, or have students assess their peers' work."
"We administer other assessments that take up so much of our time, such as screeners that are administered three times a year."	"Rethink administering screeners three times a year. Instead, use evidence from end-of-year assessments (including screeners) to inform beginning-of-year differentiation and supports. If students are new to the school or district, then administer the beginning-of-year screener. Skip the mid-year screener, and instead use classroom-based assessments to identify students who may be at risk."

Grades

Another topic that will inevitably emerge, and that must be anticipated and addressed, is grading. There are two misunderstandings about assessment and grading in schools (Marzano, 2018).

1. **The first misunderstanding is that instruction is distinct from assessment:** For example, "I taught the content for a week, and then I gave students a test." In our experience, there is an unfortunate reluctance to assess students during the course of instruction, perhaps because teachers feel that they are unqualified to craft a valid assessment and believe that the informal evidence gathered during the course of instruction is unreliable and invalid to inform teaching and impossible to use when assigning grades. This is simply not the case. We recommend that teachers and students move from assessment *of* learning to assessment *for* learning and even assessment *as* learning (Chappuis & Stiggins, 2016).

2. **The second misunderstanding is that assessing for instruction and assessing for the purpose of determining a grade are distinct:** In fact, assessment is assessment, and the information gathered during both informal and formal assessments can be used for a variety of important purposes. Grades should reflect what students learn, not how many points that they earn. Many schools, particularly secondary schools, continue to use grades that are calculated based on the number of points that students have accumulated. These points may be earned through completing homework, participating in class, or completing extra credit assignments, in addition to their performance on assessments of standard-mastery. This practice is incompatible with a mission statement that embraces the idea that all students will master prioritized standards. When points are earned simply for the completion of work or tasks, it is possible for students who do not adequately demonstrate mastery on assessments to pass a class. Alternatively, when points come from sources unrelated to mastery of standards, it is possible for students to fail even when they have mastered content by the end of the grading period.

An option to improve the accuracy, transparency, and fairness of grading is to implement standards-based grading practices. See Schimmer (2016) for a detailed description of these practices. The characteristics of standards-based grading include the following.

- Clear learning targets and success criteria

- Assessments aligned to learning targets

- Formative assessments that provide feedback to students and teachers prior to a summative assessment

- Feedback aligned to learning targets and reported in proficiency levels (not percentages)

- Opportunities to demonstrate growth in understanding

- Grades that authentically reflect what they know (not how they got there)

School leaders must start by discussing the purpose of grading, grades, and report cards in their schools. Standards-based grading is not an essential element of MTSS, but the principles and practices between them are complementary. MTSS requires that everyone has timely and accurate information about student needs and that reteaching, relearning, and reassessing options exist. Standards-based grading also includes these elements.

MTSS and RTI are directly related to mastery learning (Guskey, 2010) and to the seminal work of Benjamin Bloom (1968, 1974, 1984). Not all students learn at the same rate or respond to the same first, best instruction. Mastery learning, MTSS, and RTI anticipate and proactively prepare for this reality. Granted, MTSS-based practices inevitably raise the issue of fairness. Some teachers express the belief that it is unfair to other students—students who passed the test the first time—when we allow students multiple opportunities to show what they know. And some teachers feel that we are not teaching responsibility when we allow multiple opportunities.

Understand that educators have an important decision to make, because a firm commitment to all students learning at high levels and a firm commitment to giving students only one chance to demonstrate that learning are entirely incompatible. We all recognize, as parents, caregivers, and teachers, that students rarely learn at the same rate and in the same manner. To terminate instruction at an arbitrary date and suggest that learning of that content is at an end, and the one-time opportunity to demonstrate mastery has passed, defies all logic. But what about teaching responsibility? It is our position that responsibility is better taught by demanding that students persevere until they succeed than by giving them only one chance at success. What are we teaching students when we communicate that they don't have to actually learn the content being assessed once they've failed that first test—that they are off the hook and need not keep trying? Does it not teach responsibility when we demand that students keep up with the new content *and* receive additional support on the old content until they reach the level of understanding needed for them to be successful? We are teaching perseverance; we are insisting that they learn how to learn, and continuously strive to improve.

Colleges and universities increasingly embed multiple layers of supports for students—and those that do have higher student retention (Civitas Learning, 2019). Some careers provide multiple opportunities to enter professions: multiple chances to pass the state teaching exam; multiple opportunities to pass the bar; multiple opportunities to revise the thesis or dissertation. It is not easy, and it takes collaborative action to design a system that provides remediation and allows for additional chances to take assessments.

If educators persevere in assessing for mastery and in supporting students who have not yet demonstrated mastery, they will increasingly guide students to success. They may, for example, recognize during the process that students' difficulties with demonstrating mastery of content reveal something about the method of instruction; adjusting instruction, even for one student, may make the difference. Or they may realize that some students *do* understand the concept and content, but cannot express their mastery in the form in which they are being assessed. For example, an oral examination may need to replace the written one.

This is not to suggest that we will not hold those students and ourselves accountable for improved written expression, but if the learning target is related to identifying cause and effect in a story or analyzing the process of meiosis, the manner in which the students meet the learning target is of secondary importance. Lastly, a student's repeated inability to master a concept on a test may help educators diagnose a more fundamental need, perhaps an auditory processing deficit or a challenge with short-term memory. Assessments, from screeners to common formative assessments to diagnostics, are essential in MTSS; we must know students' specific needs in a timely manner. Once that need is discovered, staff can provide students with targeted support, and subsequent instruction and assessment will result in more success. See table 4.4 for ideas of how to respond to pushback about assessment fairness.

TABLE 4.4: RESPONDING TO COMMON ASSESSMENT FAIRNESS PUSHBACK

Possible Pushback	Possible Response
"Standards-based grading is too hard and takes too much time."	"Teachers with experience with standards-based grading report that these practices actually save time fairly shortly after initiating them, typically in the first year."
"It's not fair to give some students more time than others to learn material."	"If we are truly committed to all students learning and developing the skills needed to be future ready, then the date by which they demonstrate learning must be a variable."
"Students won't try if the assignment or assessment doesn't count as a grade on the first attempt."	"Students will be motivated to complete formative assignments and assessments when they receive feedback on this work that will help them on the summative assessment. We still record and report completion status on formatives for students and parents to see."

Resource Shortages

Often, a school does not possess the resources to successfully implement MTSS-based practices. What can you do? To anticipate or address resource shortages, school leaders can do the following.

- Inventory the resources you have on site—the human, material, and temporal resources—in other words, leaders must analyze how the people, programs, and time that are available are being utilized.

- Review where the school's money goes. Every dollar must be considered an instructional dollar. School leaders should ask, "Are we using our money as close to students as possible?" For example, are there staff members who could be working with students but who are instead completing duties that could be completed by others? We recommend considering reassigning such a staff member to work directly with students. This may necessitate hard decisions, but they are decisions that must be made. Schools are unlikely to receive more money or time in the near future, so leaders must utilize their dollars in a wiser, more efficient manner.

- Review what the school already possesses that is not being utilized or (due to insufficient training) is not being used optimally. That includes what is on shelves and in closets. In our experience, schools do not often have to spend new money for programs; there are often research-based programs already available that can be reintroduced or revitalized. Leaders must inventory these programs.

Leaders must rethink the way their colleagues' skills are being utilized if they are going to meet the differentiated needs of all students. See table 4.5 for ideas of how to respond to pushback about resource shortages.

Summary

The difference between success and a slow, painful death for any new initiative is significantly impacted by the systems that are in place to monitor and sustain those efforts. The steps to success described in this chapter will ensure that the structures exist to support school teams in their journey. The next chapter discusses the critically important topic of evidence. Without evidence, we do not know if students are adequately responding to supports, and we do not know if our supports as a whole are positively impacting all students. Moreover, evidence can be a motivator. When students, families, and staff members see evidence of success, we are more likely to persevere and commit to future learning.

TABLE 4.5: RESPONDING TO COMMON RESOURCE SHORTAGE PUSHBACK

Possible Pushback	Possible Response
"We don't have enough programs to meet student needs."	"Consider three truths: (1) people make the difference, not programs; (2) we have found that, with professional learning and practice, we can use our existing programs better; and (3) there are free or very low-cost programs we can use to meet students' needs."
"There just aren't enough staff to meet student needs."	"We agree. We have never been in a school with more staff to serve students than there are students to serve. Therefore, we need to prioritize supports for those students most in need, efficiently and strategically schedule staff for Tier 3 interventions, and take full advantage of the power of teachers and teacher teams to provide Tier 1 and 2 supports."
"We don't have enough time for this extra work."	"We agree. Therefore, we must courageously examine how we are currently spending our time so that we carve out time for the supplemental supports that some students desperately need to be successful."

Steps to Success for MTSS-Based Practice

Look at the steps to success in the Step column. Considering your school's current goals, record potential places where you might receive pushback (including the tight-loose debate, behavior instruction differences, assessment, grading disagreements, and resource shortages) or encounter other obstacles, and then brainstorm actions your team might take to avoid or address those.

Step	Potential Pushback Source or Obstacle	Potential Response to Pushback	Potential Obstacle Response or Workaround
1. Clearly define the desired outcomes and establish completion dates.			
2. Identify key interim and final benchmarks.			
3. Research and identify the information, resources, and professional learning necessary to meet the interim and final benchmarks.			

page 1 of 2

4. Acquire and distribute the required information and resources and provide the professional learning.	5. Anticipate and prepare for roadblocks and obstacles.	6. Initiate the MTSS-based practices.	7. Gather and analyze evidence.	8. Make midcourse corrections.	9. Provide targeted and positive supports to teams and individuals. 10. Persevere, measure, and celebrate success.

Inventory Tool for Assessments

What information do we need?	What assessments do we administer?	Are there redundancies?	Are there gaps?

CHAPTER 5

What Does Student Evidence Reveal?

All journeys need evidence to inform progress. When taking a trip by car, we rely on data from our gas gauge to help us determine when we need to fuel up. Although most of us now use turn-by-turn GPS apps, our odometers can help us determine how far we have gone and how far we still need to go. A car's tachometer tells us how hard our car's engine is working, and its warning lights give us other important information. MTSS needs its own evidence to drive toward success.

The journey to MTSS implementation has, up to this point, been based on evidence of a school's needs and current plans. The guidance that we have provided is based on the research and best practices in the area of MTSS and our own experience in leading schools and districts. This chapter describes the types of evidence that school teams need to actively gather, analyze, and utilize to continuously improve. School decisions can and should be driven by the timely evidence that we produce.

Data Types by Need

Initiatives cannot be judged successful simply because we implement them; they must positively impact student learning and outcomes. Frequent, accurate, and appropriate information about the efficacy of initiatives is required to justify the effort needed to sustain them. This requires access to balanced evidence, provided through formal and informal assessments; these data are the engine that drives education and MTSS.

A useful example of the importance of balanced data comes from the evidence we, as educators, might gather when providing students with intensive intervention. For a student receiving comprehension supports, we gather progress-monitoring data to determine the extent to which he or she is making progress with the specific skills that are the focus of the intervention—evidence of reading comprehension, in this case. We need to balance this evidence with additional evidence we gather about how this progress transfers to the classroom. Is the student performing better in core classrooms? Is the student participating more and completing more work? Does the student appear more motivated and confident? A balance of evidence helps us avoid drawing incorrect conclusions about the progress that is (or is not yet) being made.

A balanced set of evidence compiled through evidence-gathering tools includes those that do the following.

- **Identify students with significant gaps in foundational behavioral and academic prerequisite skills:** Commonly gathered through screeners.

- **Determine the extent to which students are responding to core content:** Commonly gathered through common assessments and surveys (completed by teachers or students).

- **Identify the causes or prerequisite skills that most frequently contribute to student difficulties:** Commonly gathered through diagnostics.

- **Determine the extent to which students are responding to Tier 2 and Tier 3 interventions:** Commonly gathered through progress monitoring.

Educators must ensure they are gathering, analyzing, and utilizing evidence to inform and impact student learning. They must avoid using data as a hammer to simply rank and sort students and start using data as a flashlight (to shine the light on the evidence the data are revealing).

We suggest that schools gather evidence that functions as described in table 5.1.

Identifying and administering assessments is not enough. Teams must ensure that they are gathering, analyzing, and utilizing evidence garnered from assessments to inform teaching practices and impact student learning. Table 5.2 (page 100) describes various types of student evidence.

Frequent data analysis, at both the grade- and content-level team and schoolwide levels, is fundamental to MTSS-based practices. Schools must have systems in place that do the following. For example, collaborative teams discuss data from common assessments and use them to inform their supports for individual students,

TABLE 5.1: DATA TYPES AND GATHERING METHODS

What the Data Should Do	How Such Data Are Gathered	Example of Such Data
Identify students with significant gaps in foundational behavioral and academic prerequisite skills.	Screeners	This may take the form of reading tests administered to all students or an examination of attendance and behavioral data from the preceding year.
Determine the extent to which students are responding to core content.	Common assessments and surveys (completed by teachers or students)	This evidence comes from the common assessments that teams administer and from the self-assessment surveys of a classroom's climate that students complete.
Identify the causes or prerequisite skills that most frequently contribute to student difficulties.	Diagnostics	This may be as simple as reading with a student to listen for his or her fluency and accuracy and for patterns of errors, or it may be a more formal mathematics diagnostic that asks students a series of increasingly difficult problems to identify where needs exist and where supports should begin.
Determine the extent to which students are responding to Tier 2 and Tier 3 interventions.	Progress monitoring	This evidence comes from the readministration of the portion of the common assessments that revealed the Tier 2 need in the first place and through administering the short progress-monitoring probes that come with intensive intervention programs or through external validations of progress (such as an oral reading-fluency probe to measure reading progress).

whole classes, whole grade levels, and whole courses. There must be a communication system in place to share data with MTSS teams so that they can identify students who are repeatedly experiencing difficulty on assessments and initiate timely additional supports.

TABLE 5.2: TYPES OF STUDENT EVIDENCE

	Screeners	Common Assessments and Surveys	Progress Monitoring	Diagnostics
Why?	Identify students with significant needs in foundational skills	Determine the efficacy of core Tier 1 instruction	Determine the efficacy of interventions; determine the extent to which students are responding to intervention	Determine why a student is experiencing difficulties; examine the specific areas in which the student most needs support
Who?	All students	All students	Students receiving supplemental supports	Students not yet responding to instruction and intervention; students about whom we need additional information
How often?	At least annually, often three times per year	Short cycle; several times per unit	Every week or two weeks	As often as needed to inform supplemental supports

What does it assess?	Broad domains	Essential content	The skills or targets with which students are receiving more time and alternative supports (Tier 2); the domain in which the student is receiving support (Tier 3)	Specific, prerequisite skills which are likely contributing to difficulties
On which students or groups does it focus?	All students	Students in a grade level, course, or class	Students receiving supports in small groups	Individual students
What does it inform?	Tier 3 supports; scaffolds required for students to access Tier 1 content	Tier 1 and 2 supports	Tier 2 and 3 supports	Tier 3 (and perhaps Tier 2) supports
How is it used?	Identify which students require the most intensive supports; determine who will require significant scaffolds to access core content.	Determine a team's success in ensuring students master prioritized content; enable teams to learn from one another about effective practices; identify students who require more time and alternative supports to master essential content; identify the skills with which all students, and specific students, require more time and alternative supports.	Validate the efficacy of interventions; ensure that students are responding to interventions.	Determine which supports will most target student needs.

The reproducible "Five Questions of MTSS" (page 111) provides a quick resource educators can use to identify and discuss any students who might be at risk and the rationale that supports their concern.

Screeners

Universal screening is a popular MTSS term. What does it mean? Universal screening, or screeners, filter those students who are at high risk of failure unless they receive immediate, targeted, and intensive supports. We can predict who these students are—they scored in the lowest performance band on the state test; they scored in the 6th percentile on a norm-referenced test; they were suspended for twelve days last year.

Screening approaches should satisfy three criteria. First, they must clearly distinguish individuals who require intervention. Practicality is the second criterion for an ideal screening mechanism and requires that the process be brief and simple enough to be implemented reliably. Educators must perceive the effort to screen as reasonable and not onerous. Third, an ideal screening system must have a net positive effect; students identified as at risk for failure receive timely and effective interventions (Kettler, Glover, Albers, & Feeney-Kettler, 2014).

As an example, consider a student being screened in the behavior domain. Schools and teachers may screen all students in the area of internalizing and externalizing behaviors using the following.

- Philadelphia Urban ACE Survey (Public Health Management Corporation, 2013)

- Student Risk Screening Scale—Internalizing and Externalizing (SRSS-IE; Ci3T, 2020; Drummond, 1994)

- Student Risk Screening Scale (SRSS) and Student Internalizing Behavior Screening Scale (SIBSS; Cook et al., 2011)

The SRSS asks staff to rate a student's frequency of displaying behaviors such as peer rejection, negative attitude, and aggressive behavior. The SIBSS asks staff to rate a student's frequency of displaying behaviors, including feeling nervous or fearful, being bullied by peers, or feeling withdrawn.

There are many academically based screeners as well, such as the following.

- Dynamic Indicators of Basic Early Literacy Skills (DIBELS), a free elementary reading screener

- i-Ready assessments for mathematics and reading from Curriculum Associates (requests fee; www.curriculumassociates.com)
- Star Assessments for mathematics and reading from Renaissance Learning (requests fee; www.renaissance.com)

Completed at the conclusion of a school year by staff who know students well, data from these screeners could be leveraged to provide supports to students at the very beginning of the next school year, before another year of difficulties is allowed to occur. They require little time to complete, and students with behavioral needs above a given threshold will very likely require immediate, positive, and structured behavioral support at the start of the following year to be successful.

Consider these additional notes on screeners.

- **While there may be value in using formal assessments as screeners at the beginning of the school year, professional educators are highly qualified to screen students toward the *end* of a school year:** In this way, educators use evidence they have gathered throughout a school year in preparation for the next year. This is so the next school year begins with immediate supports in place for the most vulnerable students. For example, the fourth-grade team meets toward the end of the year to identify the students most at risk in literacy, numeracy, and behavior, as well as to detail these students' difficulties and review strategies or approaches that yielded positive results. After serving students for the entire year, these fourth-grade teachers are more than qualified to complete this screening process. What could be done with the information that this team gathered? It could and should be shared with fifth-grade teachers so that the fifth-grade team begins the year with positive, differentiated practices in place for screened students. This ensures students successfully access content and receive Tier 1 and Tier 2 supports that allow them to master essential concepts and skills. The school's leadership and MTSS teams can ensure that screened students receive timely, targeted, and intensive Tier 3 supports (that are hopefully an extension of the impactful Tier 3 supports that were provided during the previous year).

- **It's possible that screeners, whether through the administration of assessment screeners or processes, need not be conducted three times a year:** We have had success screening only at the end of the year, in preparation for initiating supports for students in need at the very beginning of the next year. For this reason, we argue that screening needs only to take place at the end of a school year in preparation for the next year. Exceptions would, of course, exist for students new to the school district and students first entering schools (typically incoming kindergarten students). For all other students, we contend that mid-year and beginning-of-year screening would not provide more value than the quantitative and qualitative evidence gathered from all students in a year. This is provided that teacher judgment is valid and school assessments are reliable.

Common Assessments

A common assessment, or common formative assessment, can be defined as any assessment collaboratively created (or selected), and given by two or more teachers with the intention of collaboratively examining the results for shared learning, instructional planning for individual students, and modifications to curriculum, instruction, or assessment. They are teacher-created (or teacher-selected), teacher-owned assessments that are collaboratively scored and that provide immediate feedback to students and teachers. Larry Ainsworth (2015) with Donald Viegut suggests:

> Common formative assessments [provide] regular and timely feedback regarding student attainment of the most critical standards ... [and] also foster consistent expectations and priorities in a grade level, course, and department regarding standards, instruction, and assessment. ... Most importantly, common formative assessment results enable educators to diagnose student learning needs accurately in time to make instructional modifications. (pp. 95–96)

Research consistently shows that these assessments significantly and positively impact student learning (Graham, Hebert, & Harris, 2015). As we assess how students are progressing toward mastering the identified priority standards, evidence from common assessments reveals to teachers where they need to differentiate and adjust instruction to ensure this outcome is met.

Common assessments are constructed to assess the key learning outcomes of priority standards, the same priority standards mentioned earlier in the book. To be useful and valid, these assessments must meet several criteria (Ainsworth, 2015).

1. A proficient score must accurately indicate that a student has learned.

2. A low score should indicate that a student needs additional support.

3. Analyses of errors must help collaborative teams efficiently determine student needs and target teaching for students who have not yet demonstrated mastery of essentials.

Collaborative analyses of results by teams can inform future practice. As they collaborate, they must investigate and discuss the answers to the questions in figure 5.1.

Specifically, teams will know the following information.

- To what extent did the team guide all students toward mastery?
- What concepts or skills need to be reviewed with the entire class?
- What factors have contributed to student difficulties?
- What additional strategies/resources are needed to ensure students improve their mastery?
- What patterns can be identified from student errors?
- Among collaborative team members, which instructional strategies proved to be most effective?
- Among collaborative team members, which instructional strategies proved not to be effective?
- How can the assessment be improved?
- Which students need more time and an alternative approach to master priority standards?
- With which standards and skills do these students need more time and an alternative approach?

Figure 5.1: Teacher team questions regarding common assessments.

*Visit **go.SolutionTree.com/schoolimprovement** for a free reproducible version of this figure.*

Teams' analyses must lead to planning the supplemental supports that some students will need. This planning will address the questions in figure 5.2.

Specifically, teams will know the following information.

- What reteaching will be provided to these students so that they progress in their mastery of essentials?
- When will this reteaching be provided?
- Who will provide this reteaching (and who will provide the enrichment opportunities to students who have demonstrated mastery)?
- What strategies or resources will be used during this reteaching?
- How will student progress be monitored to measure the effectiveness of this reteaching?

Figure 5.2: Supplemental support planning.

*Visit **go.SolutionTree.com/schoolimprovement** for a free reproducible version of this figure.*

Teacher teams drive Tier 2 of MTSS, and common assessment evidence to inform instruction can lead to incredibly dramatic gains in student learning (Black & Wiliam, 1998; Bloom, 1984; Hattie, 2009, 2012; Hattie & Clarke, 2019; Meisels et al., 2003; Rodriguez, 2004). Tier 2 means more time and additional supports for students to master the essentials that were taught in Tier 1. Therefore, it's teacher teams that work together to plan and deliver Tier 2 supports, given that they are the experts in the grade level or course. While teachers on the team can and will collaborate with each other to determine the alternative strategies that will best serve students who have not yet demonstrated mastery of the essentials, the teams take primary responsibility for Tier 2.

When individual students are found to have not demonstrated the levels of mastery that the teams expect—in other words, when Tier 2 supports are required—we recommend that teachers augment the collaborative teams with the reproducible "Tier 2 MTSS Questions" (page 112).

Diagnostics

Diagnostic assessments identify a student's needs in relation to the content or domain in which the student has difficulties. They are administered to students who are at risk on an individual basis. There are formal and informal diagnostics. An example of a formal diagnostic would be a comprehensive phonics inventory. An example of an informal diagnostic would be an analysis of the errors a student made when completing an open-ended mathematics test. These assessments provide specific and in-depth information that assists in targeting the interventions that allow students to close gaps in their learning. When thinking of the type of diagnostic to use, consider the reason why we, as educators, administer diagnostics. We do not administer diagnostics to find out what is wrong with a student or to label the deficit; we conduct a diagnostic to determine which targeted supports we need to provide. While screeners may provide additional information regarding student needs, their purpose is to identify students who are at risk. The purpose of diagnostics is different.

While a diagnostic's relative length likely precludes their administration to all students, it serves an essential purpose in assisting educators in planning targeted and effective instruction and interventions. The use of diagnostics should be restricted to when they can provide either new or more reliable information about a student's academic or behavioral needs. It is important to weigh the potential value of the information that could be mined against the time required to administer a comprehensive diagnostic test. In our experience, schools (typically at the elementary grades) sometimes use longer, diagnostic-like assessments with all students, calling these assessments *screeners*. While these assessments are valuable and fulfill a role in schools, these twenty- to thirty-minute assessments should be reserved for use as diagnostics.

A behavioral diagnostic could be a simplified functional behavioral analysis administered by a staff member to a student who has been identified with behavioral difficulties. Please check your local requirements about who can administer behavioral diagnostics; with the input of psychologists from around the United States and Canada, we created a streamlined functional behavior analysis that any staff member can complete, and its use has improved the supports we provide to students. You can find this streamlined analysis in *Behavior: The Forgotten Curriculum* (Weber, 2018). The functional behavior analysis reveals *antecedents*—reasons—that may be contributing factors to the misbehavior. If a student acts out when being asked to work collaboratively on a task involving reading, the team may conclude that the student would benefit from support and guidance in working with others or with reading. For example, if while conducting a reading running record with a student who has difficulty and a dislike for reading reveals that the student has difficulty decoding single-syllable words, the team may conclude that the student would benefit from immediate, intensive, and targeted intervention in single-syllable phonics. We do not diagnose to label a student, or exhaustively map a student's learning profile; we diagnose to determine the causal factor in a student's difficulties, and to inform the intervention that can and will be provided, not to attach a label to that student.

Progress Monitoring

Progress-monitoring assessments measure the extent to which students are responding to supplemental interventions. They also ensure that the right interventions have been chosen for a student or a group of students. Common assessments and progress-monitoring assessments share quite a few attributes. While common assessments determine all students' responses to core Tier 1 instruction (and, in alternative forms, students' responses to Tier 2 supports), progress-monitoring assessments determine the responses of at-risk students to the most intensive interventions.

Staff collect student performance data from progress monitoring on a regular basis and plot results over time, from year to year. Drawing a line of best fit through student scores provides an indication of the rate of improvement, or lack of improvement, that the student is making toward achieving mastery of specific skills.

The results of progress monitoring are shared with the teachers with whom the student works and the MTSS team. When progress is adequate, we keep doing what we've been doing. When progress is not yet adequate, particularly over several years or multiple administrations, then we consider adjustments to the offered supports, both in the core classrooms and in the interventions.

Progress monitoring is an essential tool in a well-defined MTSS practice. It assesses the adequacy of school supports as well as students' responses to these supports. Information can lead a team to conclude that a student needs a different type of support or more intensive level of support, or to decide that a student has responded to interventions and may be successful with fewer supports, so that students receive supports in the least restrictive levels.

A check-in/check-out (CICO) process is used in behavior to monitor progress— to determine if a behavior intervention is working and the extent to which students are responding to intervention. In the CICO process, the teacher team, with administrative input and guidance, identifies a behavior to monitor daily or weekly with a simple rating scale that both student and teacher can complete, with monitoring and mentoring provided by an adult with whom the student checks in and checks out. Revisions and decisions can be made regarding behavior based on CICO data just as revisions and decisions to academic supports can be made using more academic progress-monitoring tools. For examples of CICO forms, see *Behavior: The Forgotten Curriculum* (Weber, 2018).

PLC Dialogue

Evidence and data aren't only the engine of MTSS; evidence of student learning and of the efficacy of our teaching and supports is the lifeblood of PLCs. The following scenario provides an example of a collaborative team discussing evidence of learning.

A fifth-grade mathematics team gathers to talk about the results of a pretest they just administered on the topic of adding and subtracting fractions with like and unlike denominators. The results show that 30 percent of the students achieved Proficient scores, with the rest of the class scoring at the Far From Proficient level.

One of the team members had taken responsibility for collecting and charting the data, and it is available for all to see at the start of the meeting. The team members then engage in dialogue about what they see as strengths and challenges for the students. They agree that most students are able to add and subtract fractions with like denominators and about half appear to be able to find the least common multiple. The data also lead them to believe that their teaching should focus on the need to identify a common denominator when adding or subtracting fractions and finding equivalent fractions once the common denominator has been achieved.

The team establishes a goal for the unit and has determined that the percentage of students scoring at the proficient level and higher on the fraction addition and subtraction postassessment will increase from the 30 percent who did so on the pretest to 100 percent, as measured by the teacher-made fraction addition and subtraction postassessment.

The discussion shifts to instructional strategies, and the team agrees to provide extension work for students who have mastered the skill and spend extra time providing direct instruction and extra practice for students who are not yet proficient. Some suggestions they have at this stage include the following.

- Have students play a fraction addition and subtraction game online.

- Review the introductory minilesson with small groups.

- Teach the minilesson and complete practice on finding common denominators.

- Set up peer-to-peer grouping where proficient students work with those approaching proficiency, while the teacher works with the students most in need.

As the meeting time concludes, the team establishes what they will use as success criteria. They expect that the postassessment results will be significantly higher than the pretest results, as noted. They also want to observe their students conceptually representing adding fractions using visual models, to observe students going through each of the steps required to add and subtract fractions, and to ensure that they are engaged in each of the learning experiences that are built into the unit.

The ways in which this teacher team discussed evidence of learning as indicated on a common assessment in mathematics, and the way they transformed data into evidence into action, would be mirrored by the MTSS team in analyzing data of student progress in response to Tier 3 interventions. The MTSS team is guided by the "Five Questions of MTSS" (page 111) as they look at the progress of students receiving a given intervention as a whole as well as the progress of individual students when collaboratively examining evidence and planning for future actions.

Summary

Data become evidence when educators use the data to plan next steps in the teaching and learning cycle. Analyzing the data generated by each type of assessment yields key information to assist educators in planning next steps and producing a targeted plan that promotes success for all students. The comprehensive suite of assessments covered in this chapter provides the evidence required to proceed along the MTSS road map.

Five Questions of MTSS

Identify and describe any students who might be at risk of experiencing success in Tier 1 in the absence of supplemental supports. Include the rationale that supports your concern.

1. About which students do we have concerns?	
2. In which areas do we have concerns? a. Academic skills b. Behavioral skills	
3. What are we currently doing to support the student and meet the student's needs?	
4. What supports will we be providing in the future?	
5. Has the student responded to the instruction and interventions we have been providing?	

Tier 2 MTSS Questions

Teacher teams collaboratively analyze their students' successes at Tier 1 in the areas of behavior and academics as they plan the more time and alternative supports that make up Tier 2.

1. Which students have not yet mastered prioritized content?
2. With which specific skills does each student require more time and an alternative approach to gain greater mastery?
3. Why does the team believe that this specific skill has not been mastered? (May include both academic and behavioral cause)
4. What strategies does the team feel will best address this need?
5. When will these Tier 2 interventions be provided? By whom?
6. What tool will the team use to confirm that the student has progressed toward mastery of prioritized content? By when?

EPILOGUE

If there is any positive associated with the COVID-19 pandemic, it may be that there exists a heightened awareness of many of the needs that MTSS addresses, whether they be equity, social justice, trauma, or SEL—hence our need for a well-informed, well-maintained, systematic approach.

The principles of multitiered system of supports represent the most comprehensive, research-based, and logical set of procedures and practices in which schools can engage to ensure that all students graduate from high school ready for college or a skilled career. Our experiences with schools across the United States and Canada have led us to conclude that the educators in these schools embrace the notion that the principles of MTSS are both necessary and representative of the ways in which schools should be functioning. School leaders accept the research-proven effectiveness of the elements of MTSS and are increasingly seeking out specific guidance on how to begin or how to get better.

The MTSS road map is designed to provide that guidance. Through no fault of their own, school leaders may not know where to start, or what to do next, to improve their systematic supports for students. We hope that this book guides school teams through a collaborative process that nurtures a positive culture and builds the structures that support high levels of learning for every student. We recognize that all organizations, leaders, and professionals benefit from thought partners, particularly partners who understand the antecedents and evidence behind the practices they are looking to implement, and partners who have done, and are doing, the work. We will proudly and respectfully partner with any school interested in our support in utilizing this MTSS road map.

The work of MTSS can perhaps best be described as organized passion—the passionate actions that embody the collective belief that all students will learn at high levels. Moreover, MTSS represents the most comprehensive, research-based, and logical set of solutions that will ensure that students graduate from high school ready for life. There are not many educators with whom we interact who doubt the wisdom of implementing MTSS. While a few of these committed colleagues report that they still come across educators who are intimidated by the changes required to ensure that all students graduate future ready—and sometimes that intimidation can come across as reluctance toward change—most of our colleagues simply want a road map to guide them through the work. We hope that this book serves as such a guide.

CASE STUDIES

This appendix explores MTSS solutions customized for an example elementary school and secondary school. We believe in the power of models and strongly encourage school leaders to avoid the pitfalls that can sidetrack staff members when they are presented with a model that might seem to be impossible to emulate. The truth is that *every* school can successfully ensure that all students learn at high levels. From the Effective Schools Movement (Edmonds, 1979; Lezotte, 2011) to 90-90-90 Schools (Reeves, 2005) to our own experiences leading schools and districts, the concept is not new: with leadership, commitment, belief, perseverance, and passion, we can create schools that meet all students' needs. Keep in mind, however, that your mileage may vary according to your school's unique needs.

We recognize that presenting schools with the mature MTSS model of another school, a school that has spent years refining and improving its processes, is both a plus and a potential curse. Examining models is a plus because it confirms for schools that it can be done—that schools can build capacity, collaborate professionally, focus curriculum, alter schedules, repurpose staff assignments, acquire resources, administer assessments, and analyze data to improve all students' learning—all the work of MTSS. But models can provide an overwhelming negative sensation for some—a sense of gloom. Educators may feel that they lack the resources to build such a system. They may worry that they are too far away from the practices represented in the model. They may fear that they do not have the commitment or the expertise among staff to successfully transform practices. They may feel as though the model represents the *only* way in which an MTSS-based plan can be built. We acknowledge and have experienced that every school is unique in its contexts, cultures, and needs, and each school has unique gifts and can design unique and uniquely successful solutions. The liberating news is that there are many pathways toward this goal. Models are not meant to be blindly replicated. They are idea generators and samples of one school's solution.

For creating these examples, we have drawn on our direct experiences leading schools and the experiences of close colleagues, as well as research and literature from the field of MTSS (Buffum et al., 2012, 2015; Fuchs & Fuchs, 2006, 2007, 2008, 2009; Hattie, 2009, 2012; Hattie & Clarke, 2019; Hierck et al., 2011; Weber, 2018). These example schools have a long and strong history with PLCs. They recognize and embrace that there can be no MTSS without PLCs and that with PLCs, a school is well on its way to developing a comprehensive system of supports.

MTSS can be used synonymously and interchangeably with the very notion of schooling—of teaching and learning. From scheduling to staffing to assessment, from general education to special education, and from academics to behaviors, MTSS is the foundation for the operations of a school. Thus, our descriptions of example schools are fairly comprehensive, and there is overlap between the two schools.

As you explore the examples, we ask you to look at the following elements for each school that is succeeding with MTSS.

- The MTSS goals and actions
- The required problem solving and assessment solutions
- A guaranteed, viable curriculum in academics and behavior
- Bell schedule
- Intervention schedule

We believe that these practical details from a school that is successfully implementing MTSS will provide examples from which educators can learn as they launch or continue their MTSS journeys.

Example Elementary School

This section includes descriptions of the MTSS applied in a diverse elementary school in a major U.S. city. In this example school, 60 percent of students are learning English and 60 percent receive free or reduced-price lunch. While based on actual schools, this example represents a conglomerate of schools. As teams of educators from a school use these case studies to inform and inspire their work, consider the following questions.

- What are we already doing?
- Of what we're doing, what are we doing well?

- What are the gaps in our supports for students?

- What are our next steps?

Now, let's meet with an example elementary school.

MTSS Goals and Actions

Figure A.1 summarizes the goals and actions of the example elementary school.

Academics	Behaviors and Social-Emotional Skills
Tier 1	
Instructional planners prioritize essential concepts and ensure access for all learners. Equitable instructional strategies include and honor all learners. Common assessments inform instruction and reteaching.	Schoolwide (across grades and classrooms) common expectations are consistently reinforced. Desired behaviors are explicitly taught. Desired behaviors are prioritized from the domains of mindsets, social skills, perseverance, learning strategies, and academic behaviors. Executive functioning and self-regulatory behaviors that support success with short-term and long-term academic tasks are both explicitly taught and consistently embedded in content-area instruction. There is a 5:1 ratio of positive acknowledgments to negative interactions (Cook et al., 2017).
Tier 2	
Specific times, schedules, and identified personnel provide supports. Supplemental reading is taught thirty minutes twice a week, and supplemental mathematics is taught thirty minutes twice a week. Grade-level schedules are staggered to maximize the use of support personnel. Supports involve more time and alternative approaches to ensure that students master the essentials. Evidence from common assessments informs and drives these supports.	Simple diagnostic protocols ensure that staff members know what behavior to target and why the student might be misbehaving; they also ensure staff understand the antecedents of behavioral needs. Focus is on reteaching and more frequent reinforcement of common expectations. Educators identify and communicate target behavior, match strategies to target behaviors, and communicate the strategies to staff and students. The CICO process is used to mentor students and monitor the effectiveness of strategies for students needing a bit more time and an alternative strategy to behave productively.

Figure A.1: Example elementary school MTSS grid.

continued →

Tier 3	
The less essential content that students miss shifts from week to week, with one week following an A schedule for interventions and the next week following a B schedule. Programs are as follows. • Mathematics—i-Ready Growth Monitoring (Curriculum Associates, n.d.) • Phonological awareness—Fast ForWord (Carnegie Learning, n.d.) • Phonics—Read Well (Voyager Sopris Learning, n.d.) • Fluency—Read Naturally (Read Naturally, n.d.) • Comprehension—Making Connections (School Specialty, n.d.)	For students who are not responding to Tier 2 supports or have been diagnosed with intensive needs in specific areas (such as anger, trauma, motivation, or self-image), research-based interventions such as the following are used in small groups or individually. • Anger Coping (Center for Childhood Resilience, n.d.) • Cognitive Behavioral Intervention for Trauma in Schools (CBITS; Jaycox, Langley, & Hoover, 2018) • Attribution (Weiner, 2006) • Self-efficacy (Bandura, 1977) These require specific programs, and programs require provided training.

The simple illustration of a problem-solving model in figure A.2 could be superimposed in each of the sections of the MTSS grid in figure A.1. Our purpose is this: diagnosing student needs, prescribing and providing supports, and monitoring student response to these supports is a cycle of inquiry that educators complete at Tiers 1, 2, and 3 for both academics and behaviors. All collaborative teams, including teacher and MTSS teams (which all schools should have), should use the simple MTSS problem-solving model when designing, delivering, and differentiating supports to ensure that all students access and master essential content.

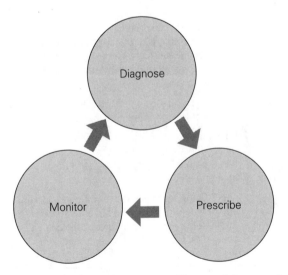

Figure A.2: Simple MTSS problem-solving model.

Assessment

The educators at this elementary school have spent years refining their use of key assessments and evidence-gathering tools and processes, as well as their data management, warehousing, organization, and use. Figure A.3 lists what assessments work best for each tier in this example school.

	Tier 1	Tier 2	Tier 3
Common assessments	Every two weeks in all content areas, including student surveys for essential behavioral skills		
Screeners			**Academics** Renaissance Star Reading (Renaissance, n.d.b) in grades 1–5 three times a year Renaissance Star Math (Renaissance, n.d.a) at the beginning and middle of the year in grades 1–5 District-created reading screeners in K–3 District-created, standards-based preassessments in reading and mathematics in grades 1–5 District-created, standards-based end-of-year assessments in mathematics in grades 1–5 **Behavior** Student Internalizing Behavior Screening Scale Student Risk Screening Scale—Internalizing and Externalizing (Ci3T, 2020; Drummond, 1994)

Figure A.3: Assessments for each tier.

continued →

	Tier 1	Tier 2	Tier 3
Progress monitoring		Alternate versions of portions of the common formative assessment CICO for behavior	i-Ready Mathematics Growth Monitoring (Curriculum Associates, n.d.) DIBELS (University of Oregon, 2021) for reading CICO or behavior intervention plan (BIP) for behavior
Diagnostics		Diagnostic interviews in phonological awareness, phonics, fluency, vocabulary, comprehension, attention, motivation, early numeracy, and overall mathematics Assistance from psychologist, speech and language pathologist, and occupational therapist for additional diagnostic supports Scales of Independent Behavior–Revised (Bruininks et al., 1996) for social and academic behaviors Functional behavioral analysis to determine the cause of a behavior and inform the creation of behavior intervention plans	
Data organization	The district has used the eduCLIMBER app and Google Suite to build data entry and reporting functions that manage, warehouse, analyze, and display data.		

Formal data and evidence are gathered using the tools listed in figure A.3. More informal and qualitative—but equally significant—evidence like student mindsets and rates of participation are entered on a weekly basis into Google Suite documents or into eduCLIMBER. The exchange of information and the problem-solving process are facilitated by the meetings and processes shown in figure A.4.

Curriculum and instruction are inextricably linked. Collaborative teams' common assessments represent the target from which teachers plan curriculum and instruction. These assessments also provide the evidence of students' learning and the efficacy of teaching that inform short-term and long-term shifts to curriculum and instruction. The next section describes the school's curriculum.

Teams and Their Meeting Frequency	What They Do
Teacher teams (Weekly)	Analyze data and complete their tasks as part of a PLC, including students' academic and behavioral data. Notes on these students are entered into eduCLIMBER or Google Suite documents by Friday afternoon. The MTSS team has access to this information, and MTSS team members collaboratively analyze evidence to determine ways to support staff and the students they serve. The teacher teams complete a form that responds to prompts like those in figures 5.1 and 5.2 (page 105).
MTSS team (Twice monthly) (Principal, assistant principals, psychologist, special education staff, counselor, speech and language pathologist, specialists, interventionists, and PLC or collaborative team representatives)	Problem solve on behalf of students who have been identified as priorities by teacher teams and the MTSS team. Priority students are those who have recently been identified as at risk or who are not adequately responding to the current levels of support. A primary responsibility of this team is to ensure that Tier 3 supports are targeted and effective. The notes from these meetings are entered into the digital platform for all internal stakeholders to review and act on.

Figure A.4: MTSS-related meetings at the example elementary school.

A Guaranteed and Viable Curriculum in Academics and Behavior

Over the past several years at this example elementary school, staff members have designed and refined instructional planners in all content areas, which are accessed on a shared online platform. The planners detail the essential standards that all students must master in the school year and in each block of instruction. Planners have been refined as analyses of student learning have revealed gaps in content or student learning. Common formative assessments have been crafted that represent the level of rigor and the format at which students must demonstrate mastery. Because these assessments include tasks that require extended responses (such as an open-ended mathematics item or a science question that requires students to draw a model), instead of only multiple-choice items, and because the school has fully embraced standards-based grading, the educators have crafted scoring guides, and they have selected anchor work from exemplary student effort, to guide the accurate grading and analysis of assessment results.

Aligning with research on behavioral skills (also known as *noncognitive factors*; Farrington et al., 2012), the school explicitly teaches, reinforces, and provides opportunities for practice, feedback, and differentiated supports in the domains of mindsets, social skills, perseverance, learning strategies, and academic behaviors, as shown in figure A.5.

Mindsets	Social Skills	Perseverance	Learning Strategies	Academic Behaviors
Students positively respond with the following types of statements. "I belong in this academic community." "My ability and competence grow with my effort." "I can succeed at this." "This work has value for me."	Interpersonal skills Empathy Cooperation Assertion Responsibility	Grit Tenacity Delayed gratification Self-discipline Self-control	Study skills Metacognition Self-regulation Goal setting	Going to class Doing homework Organizing materials Participating Studying

Source: Adapted from Farrington et al., 2012; Weber, 2018.

Figure A.5: Explicitly taught noncognitive factors in example elementary school.

Teachers provide weekly minilessons on these behavioral skills, embed the practice and reinforcement of these skills throughout the day, gather evidence of student success in displaying the behavior, and provide feedback and differentiated supports as needed. (More information on these behavioral skills is provided in chapter 5, page 97.)

Bell Schedule

The school's schedule was altered three years ago to embed one thirty-minute intervention and enrichment block once a week to provide Tier 2 supports to students in reading and enrichment opportunities (such as art, coding, and participation in the school's video production) to students already proficient in their grade level. Due to the positive impacts of these supports on student learning, the school has decided to include a thirty-minute intervention and enrichment block for Tier 2 reading and a thirty-minute intervention and enrichment block for Tier 2 mathematics in the schedule four days a week. Students are dismissed one hour early each Wednesday, when educators collaborate and engage in professional development. Figure A.6 contains the schedules, including intervention blocks, for different grade levels.

Kindergarten and First Grade	
Time	**Content**
8:00–10:00	English language arts
10:05–10:20	Recess
10:25–11:25	Mathematics
11:30–12:05	Lunch
12:10–12:40	Special or elective
12:45–1:15	Social studies
1:20–1:50	Science
1:55–2:25	Intervention and enrichment block 1
2:30–3:00	Intervention and enrichment block 2

Second and Third Grade	
Time	**Content**
8:00–9:00	Mathematics
9:05–9:35	Special or elective
9:40–9:55	Recess
10:00–12:00	English language arts
12:05–12:40	Lunch
12:45–1:15	Intervention and enrichment block 1
1:20–1:50	Intervention and enrichment block 2
1:55–2:25	Social studies
2:30–3:00	Science

Figure A.6: Schedules for different grade levels.   continued →

Fourth and Fifth Grade	
Time	Content
8:00–8:30	Social studies
8:35–9:05	Science
9:10–10:10	Mathematics
10:15–10:45	Special or elective
10:50–11:05	Recess
11:10–11:40	Intervention and enrichment block 1
11:45–12:15	Intervention and enrichment block 2
12:20–12:55	Lunch
1:00–3:00	English language arts

Students for whom Tier 3 supports are an urgent necessity—they have been determined to require intensive assistance with foundational skills—temporarily miss electives or specials, social studies, or science, or are served during independent work times when other students are engaged in differentiated practice. While students may miss time in these important content areas temporarily, until they have gotten back on track to meet grade-level expectations, they do not miss the same content each week. The intervention schedule is shifted every two weeks, moving the time during which the Tier 3 support is provided, so that while students may miss attending a certain experience, they will not miss that same experience during the following two-week cycle.

Intervention Schedule

Over the last several years, the school has inventoried the allocation of all human resources, attempting to ensure that personnel spend as much time providing direct supports to students as possible. They simply examined the schedules of all paraprofessionals and special education staff to see if and how a thirty-minute period in one of these staff members' schedules existed or could be repurposed to provide direct supports to small groups of students. Every thirty-minute period represents another small group of learners at risk whose significant needs can be met. This resulted in repurposing classroom assistants and one member of the office staff.

To help assistants work more efficiently, the interventionists provide Tier 3 supports in an unused classroom in which there are four small-group work stations. Students come to the classroom instead of the interventionists traveling to classrooms; this efficiency allows more small-group supports to take place in the day and allows students from multiple classrooms to be served in the same small group at the same time. These interventionists also travel from classroom to classroom to provide targeted, small-group Tier 1 and 2 supports to students. Teachers have staggered the start times of their instructional blocks to allow this to occur (as shown in figure A.6, page 123). The office staff has been reduced from three to two members; the third member of the previous office staff was retrained to become an interventionist. The workload of the office was streamlined through technology, more efficient processes, and by shifting responsibilities among administrative and teaching staff.

The school now utilizes four interventionists. These interventionists provide small-group supports during Tier 1 English language arts and mathematics instruction, Tier 2 supports during the intervention and enrichment block, and targeted Tier 3 supports to students most at risk. The same interventionist meets with multiple small groups throughout the day, approximately every thirty minutes, four or five days a week. A week's roster for students requiring Tier 3 support is included in figure A.7, and a daily schedule for one of the interventionists is provided in figure A.8 (page 126).

Interventionist **Mrs. Harrison** *Phonological Awareness*	Interventionist **Mrs. Harrison** *Fluency*	Interventionist **Mrs. Harrison** *Advanced Phonics*
Jason (grade 1) Erin (K) Bella (grade 1) Sadie (K) Anahi (K) Summer (K)	Brenda (grade 5) Anthony (grade 4) Stephanie (grade 5) Isabel (grade 4) Jocelyn (grade 4)	Angel (grade 5) Sergio (grade 4) Marisol (grade 5) Dominique (grade 4) Antonio (grade 5) Daniel (grade 5)
Interventionist **Mr. Gregory** *Phonics Awareness*	Interventionist **Mr. Gregory** *Fluency*	Interventionist **Mr. Gregory** *Phonics*
Logan (grade 1) Abraham (grade 1) Marisol (grade 1) Zoe (grade 1)	Jerrod (grade 5) Vanessa (grade 4) Jorge (grade 3) Ariana (grade 4) Jason (grade 3) Azucena (grade 4)	Jason M. (grade 5) Anahi (grade 4) German (grade 5) Dulce (grade 5) Jason R. (grade 4) Samantha (grade 4) Ornar (grade 5) Jasmine (grade 4)

Figure A.7: Roster for Tier 3 supports.

continued →

Interventionist Mrs. Cooper *Phonics* Saul (grade 3) Lucas (grade 2) Isaiah (grade 3) Blake (grade 3) Brittany (grade 2) Natalie (grade 2)	n/a	**Interventionist Mrs. Cooper** *Phonics* Lupe (grade 5) Lesley (grade 4) Daysi (grade 5) Maite (grade 5) Jesus (grade 5) Fabiola (grade 4)
Interventionist Mrs. Cooper *Comprehension* Eric (grade 2) Daysi (grade 3) Juan (grade 1) Christian (grade 2) David (grade 2) Stephanie (grade 1) Yareth (grade 1) Ian (grade 2)	**Interventionist Mrs. Cooper** *Phonics* Estefania (grade 3) Alexis (grade 4) Natalie (grade 3) Francisco (grade 3) Elvis (grade 4) Anayeli (grade 3)	n/a
Interventionist Mrs. Barquer *Phonological Awareness* Logan (grade 1) Abraham (grade 1) Marisol (grade 1) Zoe (grade 1)	**Interventionist Mrs. Barquer** *Numeracy* Saul (grade 5) Johnny (grade 5) Brittany (grade 4) Jennifer (grade 5) Lexandra (grade 4) Marleni (grade 5)	**Interventionist Mrs. Barquer** *Comprehension* Saray (grade 5) Jerry Lee (grade 4) Amayrani (grade 4) Kim (grade 5) Kevin (grade 4)

Times	**Focus**	**Program**	**Location**
8:00–8:30 a.m.	Tier 1 ELA—Mrs. Wilson (grade 4)		Room 123
8:30–9:00 a.m.	Tier 1 ELA—Ms. Norgren (grade 5)		Room 125
9:00–9:30 a.m.	Tier 1 ELA—Mr. Beyer (grade 3)		Room 114
9:30–10:00 a.m.	Tier 3 phonics	Read Well	Room 212
10:25–10:55 a.m.	Tier 1 mathematics—Mrs. Pedersen (grade 2)		Room 105
10:55–11:25 a.m.	Tier 1 mathematics—Mrs. Marshall (grade 3)		Room 116
11:30 a.m.–12:00 p.m.	Tier 3 fluency	Read Naturally	Room 212
12:45–1:15 p.m.	Tier 3 fluency	Read Naturally	Room 212
1:20–1:50 p.m.	Tier 3 comprehension	Making Connections	Room 212
1:55–2:25 p.m.	Tier 2 ELA (grade 2)		Room 105
2:30–3:00 p.m.	Tier 2 mathematics (grade 2)		Room 105

Figure A.8: Interventionist's schedule.

Example Secondary School

Secondary schools can efficiently and effectively systemize supports for all students, just as elementary schools can. More than 55 percent of students at this fictional secondary school detailed in this section are classified as English language learners, and more than 45 percent are eligible for free or reduced-price meals.

As teams of secondary educators from a school use this section's case study to inform and inspire their work, again consider the following questions.

- What are we already doing?
- Of what we're doing, what are we doing well?
- What are the gaps in our supports for students?
- What are our next steps?

Now, let's meet with an example secondary school.

MTSS Goals and Actions

Figure A.9 summarizes the goals and actions of this example secondary school.

Academics	Behaviors and Social-Emotional Skills
Tier 1	
Instructional planners for each course prioritize essential concepts and ensure access for all learners.	Schoolwide (across grades and courses) common expectations are consistently reinforced.
Equitable instructional strategies include and honor all learners.	Desired behaviors are explicitly taught.
Standards-based assessment and grading principles and practices are implemented.	Desired behaviors are prioritized from the domains of mindsets, social skills, perseverance, learning strategies, and academic behaviors.
Courses are co-planned and co-taught (between one general education and one special education teacher) when there are clusters of students with special needs in a class.	Executive functioning and self-regulatory behaviors that support success with short-term and long-term academic tasks are both explicitly taught and consistently embedded in content-area instruction.
All teacher teams have common assessments that inform instruction and reteaching.	There is a 5:1 ratio of positive acknowledgments to negative interactions (Cook et al., 2017).
Students learn Cornell notetaking and use it in all classrooms.	
Literacy and nonfiction writing occurs across all content areas.	

Figure A.9: Example secondary school MTSS grid.

continued →

Tier 2	
Tier 2 supports, which are targeted by the learning target, are provided during tutorials. Tier 2 supports are provided to small groups in core classes. Tier 2 supports are provided in mathematics and English support classes (in which students with significant mathematics and English needs are enrolled in addition to their core class).	Simple diagnostic protocols ensure that staff members know what behavior to target and why the student might be misbehaving; they also ensure staff understand the antecedents of behavioral needs.
	Educators identify and communicate target behavior, match strategies to target behaviors, and communicate the strategies to staff and students.
	The CICO process is used to mentor students and monitor the effectiveness of strategies for students needing a bit more time and an alternative strategy to behave productively (for students with moderate, immediate skill deficits in behavioral skills).
	Replacement behaviors (such as a student taking a timeout before they misbehave) are offered as students work toward demonstrating the expected behavior.
Tier 3	
Students who do not have individualized education plans (IEPs) receive Tier 3 supports in mathematics and English support classes. Programs are as follows. • Mathematics (i-Ready; Curriculum Associates, n.d.) • English language arts (Read 180; Houghton Mifflin Harcourt, n.d.b)	For students who are not responding to Tier 2 supports or have been diagnosed with intensive needs in specific areas (such as anger, trauma, motivation, or self-image), research-based interventions such as the following are used in small groups or individually. • Anger Coping (Center for Childhood Resilience, n.d.) • Cognitive Behavioral Intervention for Trauma in Schools (Jaycox et al., 2018) • Attribution (Weiner, 2006) • Self-efficacy (Bandura, 1977) These require specific programs, and programs require provided training. Student needs are informed through a functional behavioral analysis and receive a designed BIP.

These require specific programs, and programs require readily available training. The information gleaned from data and evidence again drives the simple problem-solving model that the school applies to each section of the MTSS model: diagnose, prescribe, and monitor progress (as shown in figure A.2, page 118). Teams use this process to design, deliver, and differentiate supports to ensure that all students access and master essential content.

Assessment

This example secondary school has refined its use of key assessments and evidence-gathering tools and processes, as well as its management, warehousing, organization, and use of data. Assessments for each tier are listed in figure A.10.

	Tier 1	Tier 2	Tier 3
Common formative assessments	Every unit in all content areas for academics Frequent mindset and learning environment self-assessment and student surveys to inform the success of behavioral instruction		
Screeners			Student Risk Screening Scale—Internalizing and Externalizing (Ci3T, 2020; Drummond, 1994) and Student Internalizing Behavior Screening Scale (Cook et al., 2011) for behavior Staff-to-staff electronic communication for all domains using eduCLIMBER and the Google Suite
Progress monitoring		Alternate versions of portions of the common formative assessment CICO for behavior	Growth monitoring checks embedded in i-Ready for mathematics and Read 180 for English language arts CICO for behavior

Figure A.10: Secondary assessment for each tier.

continued →

Diagnostics	By the student, by the learning target analysis of student needs on commonly administered assessments	Diagnostic interviews in phonological awareness, phonics, fluency, vocabulary, comprehension, attention, motivation, early numeracy, and overall mathematics Functional behavioral analysis for behaviors Assistance from psychologist, speech and language pathologist, and occupational therapist for additional diagnostic supports
Data	Use eduCLIMBER and the Google Suite to warehouse data, record notes, and aid communication with stakeholders.	

Educators gather formal data and evidence using the tools listed in figure A.10. With the data, staff exchange information and employ the problem-solving process during the meetings and processes described in figure A.11.

Team and Meeting Frequency	What They Do
Collaborative teams (Weekly)	Analyze data and complete their PLC tasks, including students' academic and behavioral data. Notes on these students are entered into eduCLIMBER or Google Suite documents by Friday afternoon.
MTSS team (Twice monthly) (Principal, assistant principals, psychologist, special education staff, counselor, speech and language pathologist, specialists, interventionists, and PLC or collaborative team representatives)	Discuss students who have been identified as priorities by teacher teams and the MTSS team. Priority students are those who have recently been identified as at risk or those who are not adequately responding to the current levels of support. A primary role of this team is to ensure that Tier 3 supports are targeted and effective. The key leader in the problem-solving and assessment process, and in the entire multitiered system of supports, is the principal. Administrators drive the process, asking key questions, holding educators accountable, and ensuring that required resources are allocated.

Figure A.11: MTSS-related meetings at the example secondary school.

Curriculum and instruction are inextricably linked. Collaborative teams' common assessments represent the target from which teachers plan curriculum and instruction. These assessments also provide the evidence of students' learning and the efficacy of teaching that inform short-term and long-term shifts to curriculum and instruction. The next section describes the school's curriculum.

A Guaranteed and Viable Curriculum in Academics and Behavior

The staff members have designed and refined instructional planners in all content areas over the past several years. The process started with a rededication to prioritizing essential learning targets. All standards are taught, but they are not taught as if they are equally important. Time has been embedded in units and the school year for assessing, using evidence from assessment to provide reteaching and enrichment (and reassessing to determine progress on specific learning targets, as necessary), and for the teaching, learning, and practice of behavioral skills (which are described in this section). Each teacher team has designed common assessments that they use to inform teaching and learning and their ongoing continuous improvement efforts.

Aligning with the school's feeder elementary school and research on behavioral skills (also known as *noncognitive factors*; Farrington et al., 2012), the school explicitly teaches, reinforces, and provides opportunities for practice, feedback, and differentiated supports in the domains of mindsets, social skills, perseverance, learning strategies, and academic behaviors like those in figure A.12.

Mindsets	• Students positively respond: ➔ "I belong in this academic community." ➔ "My ability and competence grow with my effort." ➔ "I can succeed at this." ➔ "This work has value for me."
Social Skills	• Interpersonal skills • Empathy • Cooperation • Assertion • Responsibility
Perseverance	• Grit • Tenacity • Delayed gratification • Self-discipline • Self-control
Learning Strategies	• Study skills • Metacognitive strategies • Self-regulated learning • Goal setting
Academic Behaviors	• Going to class • Doing homework • Organizing materials • Participating • Studying

Source: Adapted from Farrington et al., 2012; Weber, 2018.

Figure A.12: Explicitly taught noncognitive factors in example secondary school.

Curricular departments have taken the lead on designing minilessons on the skills that are shared and used schoolwide. All teachers provide instruction on these skills using the minilessons during homeroom, and staff have committed to reinforcing the skill of the week during the days that follow, until the next minilesson, when the process is repeated.

Bell Schedule

This secondary school shifted to an eight-period schedule to provide opportunities for students to take multiple electives or receive supplemental supports in ELA and mathematics. Figure A.13 illustrates the secondary school schedule.

Monday	
PLC Time	8:00–8:55 a.m.
Period 1	9:00–9:40 a.m.
Period 2	9:45–10:25 a.m.
Break	10:25–10:35 a.m.
Period 3	10:40–11:20 a.m.
Period 4	11:25 a.m.–12:05 p.m.
Lunch	12:05–12:40 p.m.
Period 5	12:45–1:25 p.m.
Period 6	1:30–2:10 p.m.
Break	2:10–2:20 p.m.
Period 7	2:25–3:05 p.m.
Period 8	3:10–3:50 p.m.

Tuesday Through Friday	
Period 1 or 2	8:30–9:55 a.m.
Support class	10:00–10:30 a.m.
Break	10:30–10:40 a.m.
Period 3 or 4	10:45 a.m.–12:10 p.m.
Lunch	12:10–12:45 p.m.
Period 5 or 6	12:50–2:15 p.m.
Break	2:15–2:20 p.m.
Period 7 or 8	2:25–3:50 p.m.

Figure A.13: Secondary schedule.

Students who require Tier 3 supports—for whom it has been determined that there are gaps in foundational skills that require intensive assistance—are provided this support during the support class. For example, students with significant needs in mathematics are enrolled in both a core mathematics class and a support class. Students may be deemed eligible to leave the support class when the support class teacher, core content-area teacher, and the MTSS team feel: (1) the student has sufficiently eliminated deficits in prerequisite knowledge, (2) the student is being successful in the core class (in other words, success in the support class is transferring to the core class), and (3) success will be maintained in the absence of supplemental supports. Students who are not enrolled in a support class have the opportunity to take another elective.

In the support class, the staff anticipate that students will likely have three types of needs. First, the staff predict that students with significant needs in mathematics—such that they will greatly benefit from a supplemental, companion class—may have less-than-positive mindsets about mathematics. Therefore, the support class addresses mindsets through minilessons and journal activities. Second, the staff predict that students in these classes are likely to need additional support to succeed in the core class. Therefore, the class provides preteaching and reteaching supports in collaboration with the teacher of the core class (ideally, and in many cases, the teacher of the core and support class is the same individual). Third, the staff predict that students in need of a support class may have significant deficits in essential standards from prior grade levels. Therefore, the class provides intensive, explicit, and targeted support in foundational skills from prior grade levels, based on a diagnosis of needs, using online, adaptive software with very frequent monitoring by the teacher. This plan for addressing the predictable Tier 2 and Tier 3 needs of students is replicated in English language arts classrooms.

The school also predicts that other students, whose needs are not as significant, will require Tier 2 supports. In other words, the school anticipates that not all students will learn the essentials by the end of the unit and in response to teachers' first, best instruction. The school has fully embraced and implemented principles and practices of standards-based grading. To that end, students are provided with opportunities for reteaching, relearning, and reassessment in normal class time in response to evidence gained through formative and summative assessments. As noted earlier, the rededication to prioritizing the teaching and learning of essential learning targets has provided the time for this Tier 2 support.

Intervention Schedule

Over the last several years, this school has inventoried the allocation of all human resources, attempting to ensure that personnel spend as much time providing direct support to students as possible. This has resulted in repurposing interventionists and support staff personnel. Special education staff and instructional assistants are deployed to core classes in co-taught sections and to support classes, such as the mathematics support class, to the maximum extent possible to serve students on campus with the greatest vulnerabilities. The school has also made a greater investment in the professional learning provided to instructional assistants. A typical daily roster for an interventionist is included in figure A.14 (page 134).

Time	Section	Course	Location
8:30–9:55 a.m.	Period 1 or 2	Co-Lab Mathematics II	Room K2
10:00–10:40 a.m.	Tutorial	Co-Lab Mathematics II	Room K2
10:45 a.m.–12:10 p.m.	Period 3 or 4	Mathematics I Lab	Room K9
12:10–12:45 p.m.	Lunch		Room 123
12:50–2:10 p.m.	Period 5 or 6	Mathematics II Lab	Room K2
2:10–2:20 p.m.	Break		Room 123
2:25–3:50 p.m.	Period 7 or 8	Co-Lab Mathematics I	Room K9

Figure A.14: Interventionist's schedule.

Beginning with a goal in mind establishes a clear target toward which schools can aim. We strongly recommend that schools review the case studies in this appendix and identify and learn from other schools in your region that have successfully developed systems of supports for students. The leadership of the school's MTSS team will be essential. As you do so, identify areas in which your school is relatively strong, areas for growth, and a next step.

REFERENCES AND RESOURCES

Ainsworth, L. (with Viegut, D.). (2015). *Common formative assessments 2.0: How teacher teams intentionally align standards, instruction, and assessment.* Thousand Oaks, CA: Corwin.

Akpan, B. (2020). Mastery learning—Benjamin Bloom. In B. Akpan & T. J. Kennedy (Eds.), *Science education in theory and practice: An introductory guide to learning theory* (pp. 149–162). New York: Springer.

Amabile, T., & Kramer, S. (2011). *The progress principle: Using small wins to ignite joy, engagement, and creativity at work.* Boston: Harvard Business Review Press.

Bandura, A. (1977). *Social learning theory.* Englewood Cliffs, NJ: Prentice Hall.

Bandura, A. (1994). Self-efficacy. In V. S. Ramachaudran (Ed.), *Encyclopedia of human behavior* (Vol. 4, pp. 71–81). New York: Academic Press.

Black, P., & Wiliam, D. (1998). Inside the black box: Raising standards through classroom assessment. *Phi Delta Kappan, 80*(2), 139–144, 146–148.

Blad, E. (2020). *There's pushback to social-emotional learning. Here's what happened in one state.* Accessed at www.edweek.org/education/theres-pushback-to-social-emotional-learning-heres-what-happened-in-one-state/2020/02 on February 16, 2022.

Bloom, B. S. (1968). Learning for mastery. *Evaluation Comment, 1*(2), 1–12. Los Angeles: UCLA Center for the Study of Evaluation of Instructional Programs.

Bloom, B. S. (1974). Time and learning. *American Psychologist, 29*(9), 682–688.

Bloom, B. S. (1984). The search for methods of group instruction as effective as one-to-one tutoring. *Educational Leadership, 41*(8), 4–17.

Brown-Chidsey, R., & Bickford, R. (2016). *Practical handbook of multi-tiered systems of support: Building academic and behavioral success in schools.* New York: Guilford Press.

Bruininks, R. H., Woodcock, R. W., Weatherman, R. F., & Hill, B. K. (1996). *SIB-R: Scales of Independent Behavior—Revised.* Chicago: Riverside.

Bryant, S. K. (2017). *Self-efficacy sources and academic motivation: A qualitative study of 10th graders* [Doctoral dissertation, East Tennessee State University]. Electronic Theses and Dissertations. https://dc.etsu.edu/cgi/viewcontent.cgi?article=4693&context=etd

Buffum, A., Mattos, M., & Weber, C. (2012). *Simplifying response to intervention: Four essential guiding principles.* Bloomington, IN: Solution Tree Press.

Buffum, A., Mattos, M., Weber, C., & Hierck, T. (2015). *Uniting academic and behavior interventions: Solving the skill or will dilemma.* Bloomington, IN: Solution Tree Press.

Carnegie Learning. (n.d.). *Fast ForWord.* Accessed at www.scilearn.com/program on February 15, 2022.

Center for Childhood Resilience. (n.d.). *Anger coping.* Accessed at https://childhoodresilience.org/think-first-and-anger-coping on March 21, 2022.

Centers for Disease Control and Prevention. (2022). *Understanding literacy and numeracy.* Accessed at www.cdc.gov/healthliteracy/learn/UnderstandingLiteracy.html on May 24, 2022.

Chappuis, J., & Stiggins, R. (2016). *An introduction to student-involved assessment for learning* (7th ed.). Hoboken, NJ: Pearson.

Cherng, H.-Y. S. (2017). *If they think I can: Teacher bias and youth of color expectations and achievement.* Accessed at https://hsredesign.org/wp-content/uploads/2019/04/teacher-expectations-and-high-school-outcomes-for-students-of-color.pdf on April 21, 2022.

Ci3T. (2020, September 9). *Systematic screening.* Accessed at www.ci3t.org/screening on February 15, 2022.

Civitas Learning. (2019). *What really works: A review of student success initiatives.* Accessed at https://info.civitaslearning.com/impact-report.html on February 24, 2022.

Collaborative for Academic, Social, and Emotional Learning. (2020). *CASEL's SEL framework.* Accessed at https://casel.org/casel-sel-framework-11-2020/#:~:text=The%20five%20broad%2C%20interrelated%20areas,%2C%20and%20%20responsible%20decision%2Dmaking on February 16, 2022.

Collins, J. (2001). *Good to great: Why some companies make the leap . . . and others don't.* New York: HarperCollins.

Conzemius, A. E., & Morganti-Fisher, T. (2012). *More than a SMART goal: Staying focused on student learning.* Bloomington, IN: Solution Tree Press.

Cook, C. R., Grady, E. A., Long, A. C., Renshaw, T., Codding, R. S., Fiat, A., & Larson, M. (2017). Evaluating the impact of increasing general education teachers' ratio of positive-to-negative interactions on students' classroom behavior. *Journal of Positive Behavior Interventions, 19*(2), 67–77.

Cook, C. R., Rasetshwane, K. B., Truelson, E., Grant, S., Dart, E. H., Collins, T. A., & Sprague, J. (2011). Development and validation of the Student Internalizing Behavior Screener: Examination of reliability, validity, and classification accuracy. *Assessment for Effective Intervention*, *36*(2), 71–79.

Cronin, J., & Jensen, N. (2014). *The phantom collapse of student achievement in New York*. Accessed at https://kappanonline.org/phantom-collapse-student-achievement-new-york-cronin-jensen on July 25, 202.

Cronin, J., Kingsbury, G. G., Dahlin, M., & Bowe, B. (2007, April). *Alternate methodologies for estimating state standards on a widely used computer adaptive test*. Paper presented at the American Educational Research Association, Chicago, IL. Curriculum Associates. (n.d.). *Growth monitoring*. Accessed at https://i-readycentral
.com/articles/growth-monitoring on February 15, 2022.

DeFeo, J. A. (2017). *Juran's quality handbook: The complete guide to performance excellence* (7th ed.). New York: McGraw-Hill.

DeSilver, D. (2017). *U.S. students' academic achievement still lags that of their peers in many other countries*. Accessed at www.pewresearch.org/fact-tank/2017/02/15/u-s-students-internationally-math-science on July 25, 2022.

Dell'Angelo, T. (2014). *Creating classrooms for social justice*. Accessed at www.edutopia
.org/blog/creating-classrooms-for-social-justice-tabitha-dellangelo on December 28, 2021.

DoSomething.org. (n.d.). *11 facts about high school dropout rates*. Accessed at www
.dosomething.org/us/facts/11-facts-about-high-school-dropout-rates on April 21, 2022.

Drummond, T. (1994). *The Student Risk Screening Scale (SRSS)*. Grants Pass, OR: Josephine County Mental Health Program.

Duckworth, A. L., Taxer, J. L., Eskreis-Winkler, L., Galla, B. M., & Gross, J. J. (2019). Self-control and academic achievement. *Annual Review of Psychology*, *70*, 373–399.

DuFour, R., DuFour, R., Eaker, R., Many, T. W., & Mattos, M. (2016). *Learning by doing: A handbook for Professional Learning Communities at Work* (3rd ed.). Bloomington, IN: Solution Tree Press.

DuFour, R., & Marzano, R. J. (2011). *Leaders of learning: How district, school, and classroom leaders improve student achievement*. Bloomington, IN: Solution Tree Press.

Dweck, C. S., Walton, G. M., & Cohen, G. L. (2014). *Academic tenacity: Mindsets and skills that promote long-term learning*. Seattle, WA: Bill & Melinda Gates Foundation.

Edmonds, R. (1979). Effective schools for the urban poor. *Educational Leadership*, *37*(1), 15–24.

Eller, J., & Hierck, T. (2021). *Trauma-sensitive instruction: Creating a safe and predictable classroom environment.* Bloomington, IN: Solution Tree Press.

Farrington, C. A., Roderick, M., Allensworth, E., Nagaoka, J., Keyes, T. S., Johnson, D. W., et al. (2012). *Teaching adolescents to become learners: The role of noncognitive factors in shaping school performance—A critical literature review.* Chicago: University of Chicago Consortium on Chicago School Research.

Flygare, J., Hoegh, J. K., & Heflebower, T. (2022). *Planning and teaching in the standards-based classroom.* Bloomington, IN: Marzano Resources.

Fuchs, D., & Fuchs, L. S. (2006). Introduction to response to intervention: What, why, and how valid is it? *Reading Research Quarterly, 41*(1), 93–99.

Fuchs, D., Fuchs, L. S., & Vaughn, S. (Eds.). (2008). *Response to intervention: A framework for reading educators.* Newark, DE: International Reading Association.

Fuchs, L. S., & Fuchs, D. (2007). A model for implementing responsiveness to intervention. *Teaching Exceptional Children, 39*(5), 14–20.

Fuchs, L. S., & Fuchs, D. (2008). The role of assessment within the RTI framework. In D. Fuchs, L. S. Fuchs, & S. Vaughn (Eds.), *Response to intervention: A framework for reading educators* (pp. 27–49). Newark, DE: International Reading Association.

Fuchs, L. S., & Fuchs, D. (2009). On the importance of a unified model of responsiveness to intervention. *Child Development Perspectives, 3*(1), 41–43.

Fullan, M. (2010). *All systems go: The change imperative for whole system reform.* Thousand Oaks, CA: SAGE.

Graham, S., Hebert, M., & Harris, K. R. (2015). Formative assessment and writing: A meta-analysis. *The Elementary School Journal, 155*(4), 523–547.

Guskey, T. R. (2010). Lessons of mastery learning. *Educational Leadership, 68*(2), 52–57.

Hall, C., & Mahoney, J. (2013). Response to intervention: Research and practice. *Contemporary Issues in Education Research, 6*(3), 273–278.

Hammond, Z. (2015). *Culturally responsive teaching and the brain: Promoting authentic engagement and rigor among culturally and linguistically diverse students.* Thousand Oaks, CA: SAGE.

Hanover Research. (2017). *Best practices in social-emotional learning.* Accessed at www.wasa-oly.org/WASA/images/WASA/1.0%20Who%20We%20Are/1.4.1.6%20SIRS/Download_Files/LI%202017/Sept%20-%20Best%20Practices%20in%20Social-Emotional%20Learning.pdf on December 28, 2021.

Hattie, J. (2009). *Visible learning: A synthesis of over 800 meta-analyses relating to achievement.* New York: Routledge.

Hattie, J. (2012). *Visible learning for teachers: Maximizing impact on learning.* New York: Routledge.

Hattie, J., & Clarke, S. (2019). *Visible learning: Feedback.* New York: Routledge.

Heflebower, T., Hoegh, J. K., & Warrick, P. B. (2014). *A school leader's guide to standards-based grading.* Bloomington, IN: Marzano Resources.

Hernandez, D. J. (2011). *Double jeopardy: How third-grade reading skills and poverty influence high school graduation.* Accessed at https://files.eric.ed.gov/fulltext/ED518818.pdf on May 9, 2022.

Hierck, T. (2017). *Seven keys to a positive learning environment in your classroom.* Bloomington, IN: Solution Tree Press.

Hierck, T., Coleman, C., & Weber, C. (2011). *Pyramid of behavior interventions: Seven keys to a positive learning environment.* Bloomington, IN: Solution Tree Press.

Houghton Mifflin Harcourt. (n.d.a). *iRead.* Accessed at www.hmhco.com/programs/iread#overview on February 15, 2022.

Houghton Mifflin Harcourt. (n.d.b). *Read 180.* Accessed at www.hmhco.com/programs/read-180-universal#overview on February 15, 2022.

Individuals With Disabilities Education Improvement Act of 2004, Pub. L. No. 108-446 § 300.115 (2004).

Jaycox, L. H., Langley, A. K., & Hoover, S. A. (2018). *CBITS: Cognitive behavioral intervention for trauma in schools (2nd ed.).* Santa Monica, CA: RAND Corporation.

Jenkins, J. R. (2003). *Candidate measures for screening at-risk students.* Accessed at www.nrcld.org/symposium2003/jenkins/index.html on December 28, 2021.

Kettler, R. J., Glover, T. A., Albers, C. A., & Feeney-Kettler, K. A. (2014). *An introduction to universal screening in educational settings.* In R. J. Kettler, T. A. Glover, C. A. Albers, & K. A. Feeney-Kettler (Eds.), *Universal screening in educational settings: Evidence-based decision making for schools* (pp. 3–16). Washington, DC: American Psychological Association.

Lewis, J., Asberry, J., DeJarnett, G., & King, G. (2016). *The best practices for shaping school culture for instructional leaders.* Accessed at https://files.eric.ed.gov/fulltext/EJ1120644.pdf on February 16, 2022.

Lezotte, L. W. (2011). Effective schools: Past, present, and future. *Journal for Effective Schools, 10*(1), 1–22.

Li, J.-B., Bi, S.-S., Willems, Y. E., & Finkenauer, C. (2021). *The association between school discipline and self-control from preschoolers to high school students: A three-level meta-analysis.* Accessed at https://journals.sagepub.com/doi/pdf/10.3102/0034654320979160 on March 25, 2022.

Maier, M. P., Pate, J. L., Gibson, N. M., Hilgert, L., Hull, K., & Campbell, P. C. (2016). A quantitative examination of school leadership and response to intervention. *Learning Disabilities: Research and Practice, 31*(2), 103–112.

Marzano, R. J. (2017). *The new art and science of teaching.* Bloomington, IN: Solution Tree Press.

Marzano, R. J. (2018). *Making classroom assessments reliable and valid*. Bloomington, IN: Solution Tree Press.

McTighe, J., & Wiggins, G. (2012). *Understanding by Design framework*. Accessed at https://files.ascd.org/staticfiles/ascd/pdf/siteASCD/publications/UbD_White Paper0312.pdf on March 4, 2022.

Meisels, S. J., Atkins-Burnett, S., Xue, Y., Bickel, D. D., Son, S.-H., & Nicholson, J. (2003). *Creating a system of accountability: The impact of instructional assessment on elementary children's achievement test scores*. Accessed at https://epaa.asu.edu/ojs/article/viewFile/237/363 on February 23, 2022.

Mercado, F. (2018). Whole child framework: Supporting educators in their plight toward MTSS and equity. *CLEARvoz Journal*, *4*(2), 1–14.

National Center for Learning Disabilities. (2017). *Social, emotional and behavioral challenges*. Accessed at www.ncld.org/research/state-of-learning-disabilities/social-emotional-and-behavioral-challenges on February 16, 2022.

No Child Left Behind (NCLB) Act of 2001, Pub. L. No. 107-110, § 115, Stat. 1425 (2002).

Pathways to Education. (2019). *Canada's high school dropout rates are staggeringly high, according to studies*. Accessed at www.pathwaystoeducation.ca/in-the-press/canadas-high-school-dropout-rates-are-staggeringly-high-according-to-studies-narcity/#:~:text=by%20Michelle-,Canada's%20High%20School%20Dropout%20Rates%20Are%20Staggeringly%20High%2C%20According%20To,according%20to%20Pathways%20to%20Education%3F on June 13, 2022.

Public Health Management Corporation. (2013). *Findings from the Philadelphia Urban ACE Survey*. Accessed at https://simplebooklet.com/findingsfromphiladelphiaacesurveyandcomparedacequestions on February 24, 2022.

Read Naturally. (n.d.). *Home*. Accessed at www.readnaturally.com on February 15, 2022.

Reeves, D. B. (2005). *Accountability in action: A blueprint for learning organizations* (2nd ed.). Englewood, CO: Advanced Learning Press.

Rehman, N., Mahmood, A., Ibtasam, M., Murtaza, S., Iqbal, N., & Molnár, E. (2021). *The psychology of resistance to change: The antidotal effect of organizational justice, support and leader-member exchange*. Accessed at www.frontiersin.org/articles/10.3389/fpsyg.2021.678952/full on April 21, 2022.

Renaissance. (n.d.a). *Renaissance Star Math*. Accessed at www.renaissance.com/products/star-math on February 15, 2022.

Renaissance. (n.d.b). *Renaissance Star Reading*. Accessed at www.renaissance.com/products/star-reading on February 15, 2022.

Rice, K. F., & Groves, B. M. (2005). *Hope and healing: A caregiver's guide to helping young children affected by trauma*. Washington, DC: Zero to Three.

Rodriguez, M. C. (2004). The role of classroom assessment in student performance on TIMSS. *Applied Measurement in Education*, *17*(1), 1–24.

Schimmer, T. (2016). *Grading from the inside out: Bringing accuracy to student assessment through a standards-based mindset.* Bloomington, IN: Solution Tree Press.

Schmoker, M. (2012). The problem with English language arts standards—and the simple, powerful solution. *Phi Delta Kappan, 93*(5), 68–69.

School Specialty. (n.d.). *About the program.* Accessed at https://eps.schoolspecialty.com/products/literacy/comprehension/making-connections/about-the-program#:~:text=Making%20Connections%C2%AE%20is%20a,then%20coaching%20students%20to%20independence on February 15, 2022.

Schwartz, S. (2019). *Teachers support social-emotional learning, but students in distress strain their skills.* Accessed at www.edweek.org/leadership/teachers-support-social-emotional-learning-but-say-students-in-distress-strain-their-skills/2019/07 on March 11, 2022.

Senge, P. M. (1990). *The fifth discipline: The art and practice of the learning organization.* New York: Doubleday.

Shinde, T. (2020). *To succeed, anticipate failure* [Blog post]. Accessed at https://medium.com/illumination-curated/to-succeed-anticipate-failure-64dcbcce1dea on March 8, 2022.

Souers, K., & Hall, P. A. (2016). *Fostering resilient learners: Strategies for creating a trauma-sensitive classroom.* Alexandria, Virginia: ASCD.Strauss, V. (2020, April 17). Why covid-19 will 'explode' existing academic achievement gaps. *The Washington Post.* Accessed at www.washingtonpost.com/education/2020/04/17/why-covid-19-will-explode-existing-academic-achievement-gaps on March 25, 2022.

University of Oregon. (2021). *8th edition of Dynamic Indicators of Basic Early Literacy Skills (DIBELS): Administration and scoring guide, 2021 edition.* Eugene, OR: Author.

van de Rijt, A., Kang, S. M., Restivo, M., & Patil, A. (2014). Field experiments of success-breeds-success dynamics. *PNAS Proceedings of the National Academy of Sciences of the United States of America, 111*(19), 6934–6939.

Voyager Sopris Learning. (n.d.). *Read Well.* Accessed at www.voyagersopris.com/literacy/read-well/overview on February 15, 2022.

Weber, C. (2018). *Behavior: The forgotten curriculum—An RTI approach for nurturing essential life skills.* Bloomington, IN: Solution Tree Press.

Wenger, J. (2014). *Transformational learning* [Blog post]. Accessed at https://medium.com/@johnqshift/transformational-learning-3deb1bb2e865 on April 21, 2022.

Weiner, B. (2006). *Social motivation, justice, and the moral emotions: An attributional approach.* Mahwah, NJ: Lawrence Erlbaum Associates.

INDEX

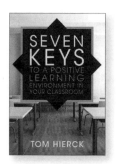

Seven Keys to a Positive Learning Environment in Your Classroom
Tom Hierck

Creating a positive classroom learning environment is a complex but necessary task. By following the seven keys the author outlines, teachers can establish clearer expectations, enhance instruction and assessment practices, and foster quality relationships with students, maximizing the potential of all students.

BKF721

Behavior Solutions
John Hannigan, Jessica Djabrayan Hannigan, Mike Mattos, and Austin Buffum

Take strategic action to close the systemic behavior gap with *Behavior Solutions*. This user-friendly resource outlines how to utilize the PLC at Work and RTI at Work processes to create a three-tiered system of supports that is collaborative, research-based, and practical.

BKF891

Uniting Academic and Behavior Interventions
Austin Buffum, Mike Mattos, Chris Weber, and Tom Hierck

Ensure students acquire the academic skills, dispositions, and knowledge necessary for long-term success. Examine what effective academic and behavior supports look like for all learners. Explore a step-by-step process for determining, targeting, and observing academic and behavior interventions.

BKF595

Demystifying MTSS
Matt Navo and Amy Williams

Demystifying MTSS distills a complex system into a customizable framework built around four fundamental components. Drawing from research and their experience in building and sustaining effective MTSS, the authors share high-leverage, practical actions school improvement teams can take to ensure all students' diverse needs are met.

BKF984

Solution Tree | Press

a division of
Solution Tree

Visit SolutionTree.com or call 800.733.6786 to order.

Wait! Your professional development journey doesn't have to end with the last pages of this book.

We realize improving student learning doesn't happen overnight. And your school or district shouldn't be left to puzzle out all the details of this process alone.

No matter where you are on the journey, we're committed to helping you get to the next stage.

Take advantage of everything from **custom workshops** to **keynote presentations** and **interactive web and video conferencing**. We can even help you develop an action plan tailored to fit your specific needs.

Let's get the conversation started.

Call 888.763.9045 today.

SolutionTree.com